Our Lives On the Line

The Air War over Vietnam
for a Navy Pilot and His Air Wing

Our Lives On the Line

The Air War over Vietnam
for a Navy Pilot and His Air Wing

A Memoir
by
Kenneth Adams

First Edition

Second Printing, August 2021

Printed in the United States of America

ISBN: 9798695395617

To The True Heroes,
The ten men in my squadron whose names
Are etched, along with more than 58,000 other true heroes,
Onto the granite panels of "The Wall,"
The Vietnam Veterans Memorial

CONTENTS

It is fatal to enter a war without the will to win it.

Douglas MacArthur

Preface

For the past 20-plus years I have given a PowerPoint presentation of the air war over North Vietnam in which I participated from 1966-1968. I was a Naval Aviator in VA-163, flying a Douglas A-4 attack aircraft. The presentation was composed of pictures that I and some of my fellow squadron pilots took as we were bombing and attacking targets in North Vietnam. They were originally Ektachrome slides that I scanned into a digital format.

There were quite a few questions as to how one can fly a single-seat airplane and take the pictures that I did. I would then explain how I did it. I started with a small camera body: a Pentax Spotmatic. My first try with the 50mm lens that came with the camera didn't give much detail since the picture was taken at a distance of several thousand feet. The solution to that was a bigger lens, which I did after saving up some money to purchase one. The 135mm Soligor lens that I purchased was in my price range but a little bigger than I would have liked. The barrel was about three inches in diameter and about five inches long. Big for the small A-4 cockpit, but it did take good pictures. I selected a focal length of infinity and secured the adjustment ring with bomb tape. I Looked through the light meter as I neared the target area, selected the appropriate F-stop and again secured the adjusting ring with bomb tape. With the camera in my right hand, my left hand flew the airplane.

We always needed full power on the airplane just to get some speed; so, using the left hand, which would normally control power, on the stick instead of the right hand, worked fine. The hardest part was using the bomb switch; the control stick was "right-handed," and the right thumb released the bombs. Getting the left thumb on the switch was a little awkward at first. The only other problem was trying to take the picture while pulling "Gs." It required a strong grip on the camera.

At launch, I would store the camera between my legs with the lens held firmly between my thighs. For landing, the only solution I had was storing the camera in the map case under the right canopy rail. It was a leather bag with an elastic band to hold it closed.

Taking this picture was easier said than done. I wanted to capture the view of an approach to a carrier landing. Just off the tail end of the carrier, to the right (otherwise known as starboard-aft), you can see the small, white outline of an F-8 that I was following.

The Author turns final to land on Oriskany. He is following an F-8 that is about to land (it appears just to the right of the ship's wake).

My first choice was for this title was *Life on the Line*. After I began reading my diary of the 1967 portion of the war, it just wasn't my life but all those in Air Wing 16. The war was controlled by Washington, and we were being sent into the most heavily defended areas in the whole world. Air Wing 16 was scheduled to fly three missions a day and each pilot would fly two of them. My diary contained the squadron number of a downed airplane, the ship number and disposition of the pilot. Every day, day after day, upon hearing the call "Pilots man your aircraft," the pilots would report to the flight deck, strap the airplanes to their butts, close the canopies and launch knowing full well this could be their last mission. We were not braver than those who fought in all the wars, but we were their equal for sure. But we had a burden that our military had never faced, we the military were being blamed for the war. At home we were greeted as baby killers, spat on and not welcomed as troops returning from war. Even East coast sailors, half a world away from the war could not leave their bases in uniform.

(Cat salute by author)

But we did our jobs none the less. We saluted the catapult officer showing our readiness to launch. With all this in mind, I changed the tile to *Our Lives on the Line*. Not only does the title represent our being there to fly our daily combat missions but also is a statement so true of our actual lives, and a very thin line it was.

4

What a Proud Day!

My dad spent money he probably didn't have to come to Texas to pin on my wings. At a small ceremony I will never forget, I became a Naval Aviator. From there I would head to Lemoore, California to check out in the A-4 Skyhawk, and other memorable events were destined to follow. Yes, this was a proud day for Dad and me; I had accomplished my goal.

PART I

Preparing for War

Never regret anything
that made you smile.

Mark Twain

Navy training for each of its aviators began with this airplane: the T-34 Mentor, a gentle but capable bird based on a Beechcraft Bonanza, an expensive craft popular at the time with doctors.

CHAPTER ONE

Growing Up

My dad and my two uncles fought in WWII, one uncle in Europe the other initially flying B-24s from North Africa and then in Italy. My dad started in India and then in Burma, near where I would be 20 years later.

I lived with my grandparents, my mom and my dad's sister on a farm in Indiana. We grew food for the Army and ourselves. Times were tight. I was about 3 ½ when grandpa took me into town and, holding my hand, told me to stand up straight because my dad would be coming home soon. It was V-J Day but that didn't mean as much to me as did my dad coming home.

It was 1946 before Dad and the others were back; in that year there was the greatest number of divorces in our country's history. The war had changed everyone and everything: soldiers, wives, jobs; and it was no different for my parents. After their divorce, my younger brother and I lived with my grandparents on the farm.

We mucked out the horse stalls and fed the horses which of course led to more mucking, helped with getting wood for the kitchen stove and the heating stove in the winter. Our bedroom was an unheated room above the kitchen, but it was large with windows for light and generally a fun room even if it was cold during the winter. Grandma always gave us a hot water bottle for our bed and life didn't seem so bad.

I think many of my squadron mates probably had similar childhoods as we were mostly mid-twenties to late 30's in age. It was a simpler time; as most of us were first born, a responsibility came with that. You were expected to become the man of the house and take care of the family if something went wrong. An expectation of responsibility meant you kept on the straight and narrow and you were expected to succeed in life.

My dad had wanted to be a pilot like his brother, especially since he was the eldest son; he had bad eyesight so being a pilot was out, but he did work his way into becoming an observer-spotter in the back seat of a Stinson L-5 aircraft in Burma. When he came back, he made model, flying planes, some of which were of his own design. This instilled in me the idea of becoming a pilot.

As I grew older, I participated in the normal sports of the day: football, wrestling and running track. Since there was no money for college, I knew I had to get a scholarship of some kind and was fortunate in that I got good grades: this enabled me to get several scholarships offers. The one from the Navy Regular ROTC program paid the most and would cut down on the number of part time jobs I would need. The Navy sent me to Miami University in Oxford, Ohio.

College was harder than I thought it would be. We were on a semester system. As a physics major, I had two, five-hour classes:

*Stinscn L-5 owned by the author. It is very much like
the one in which his father served in Burma as an observer.*

physics and math. I attended a physics lab, a three-hour Naval Science course plus lab (drill practice) and an elective three-hour course like English or Philosophy. I was a floor advisor (paid for my room) and washed dishes, pots and pans to pay for my food.

Each summer we had a midshipman cruise to learn more about our future naval career. On our first cruise we were deck sailors without any skills but learned how to chip paint, work in the boiler rooms and many other jobs accomplished by hard working sailors. It was a real eyeopener as far as what it takes to keep a ship afloat. Our second cruise we experienced the life of a marine, which was an optional career path at the end of our schooling. We went to Little Creek, Virginia where we got short haircuts (no hair). Then came the drilling and getting yelled at every second of the day.

The training was complete with a beach invasion, climbing down rope ladders hung from the side of the ship and into landing craft, the same type that were used in the "D Day" invasion. That was not a fun ride but thankfully we didn't have guns shooting at us as we hit the beach. We then went to Corpus Christi, Texas to experience life as an aviator, which was where my interest lay. I qualified to be a lifeguard at the base pool; when I wasn't flying, I worked on getting a great tan and bleached hair, which was finally growing. Such a hard life it begs the question of what choice would a reasonable person make? The third midshipman cruise was as a junior officer on a ship. I was fortunate in that I would join my ship in Italy; I got my first chance to see the world. I flew into Frankfurt, Germany with a classmate. Frankfurt was still recovering from the war, and the city still had many ruins that gave one an appreciation of the destructiveness of the war.

We both planned to buy a motorcycle to travel around Europe but soon found out that they were in short supply and expensive. We ended up with a small Fiat that could barely get out of its own way, but off we went: first around Germany then France, Spain and finally Italy where we got our ships.

I enjoyed Spain the best. Our first bull fight was something else. I had no idea about what was to happen. We got cheap seats which meant we sat on the hot sunny side with the locals who noticed we had no food or drink. They shared their food with us and taught me how to drink out of a leather bota. Such a great time.

We had planned on spending a night in Pamplona but when we arrived, there was a big festival going on, so there was nowhere to stay but a campground. Off we went with no tent or sleeping bag, but we knew we could survive. At the campground we met three Swedish guys who spoke better English than I; they explained that the festival included running with the bulls the next morning. They invited us to join them and gave us the big rule: once the flare goes off, start running, do not look back or you will get tripped and then run over by the bulls. Just keep running until you get in the stadium and you will be alright. They had some good wine to share with us, so it was a great night and fun morning.

What they didn't tell us was that some idiots want to get gored, to show their manhood, and would pile up in front of the stadium; so unless you climbed over them, you might end up with a bull horn stuck in you. I had no problem climbing over all those idiots. The Navy did not plan for me to be trampled or gored.

We ended up staying until the end of the festival. This was my first real experience developing a friendship with people from another country. One Swede was from the north country and the best way for him to converse with his southern countrymen was in English, which seemed strange to me.

My classmate was to get his ship at the French border and my ship was farther south in Italy. It fell to me to sell the car. We didn't get our money back completely, but it still was a cheap way for us to see Europe.

My ship was the *USS English* DD-696 launched in February 1944. I came aboard almost two decades later, in mid-July 1963. You might say she was an old, small destroyer and you would be correct. I was the only midshipman officer on board, so I was "rocket last," or the most junior officer onboard. Fortunately for me I did not get seasick, which is really a plus on a small rocky ship such as the *English*.

We cruised the Mediterranean Sea as an escort for a task force assigned to a carrier. This is USS English (from a Navy file photo).

We departed the Med to return to Norfolk, Virginia, her home port. On the way back we ran into a hurricane, which tossed our small ship around as if it were a cork.

The bow would take blue water—not spray but solid water— which would rush over the second, forward 5-inch-gun mount. At the same time the propellers would come out of the water to wildly shake the whole ship. We'd then teeter-totter, the front pointed to the sky and the rear deck now under water.

For several days I stood Officer of the Deck watch with the Skipper, four hours on four hours off. What a ride. And thus, ended my destroyer career.

CHAPTER TWO

The Beginning

I was commissioned an Ensign in June 1964. I was now earning a paycheck from the US Navy, $222.00 a month and $50.00 a month to pay toward my mess bill at the Bachelor Officers Quarters (BOQ) or the officers' mess aboard the ship. We did have to buy our own uniforms: a blue winter uniform, a brown aviator uniform and a white uniform for summer. My flight school entry date had been changed; as a physics major, the Navy thought it could send me to nuclear training. I fought to get back into the flight program; eventually got reassigned but had lost my initial start date. In some ways it worked out in my favor. I had an October start date, so I went temporarily to Patrol Squadron VS-56 that was flying P2V's in Norfolk Virginia.

I was assigned as the recreation officer, so I organized softball and football games for the squadron and enjoyed being in a real squadron, even if I was a gold bar, know-nothing "nugget" with no useable skill.

*Navy file photo of a P2V, the airplane flown by the author's first
temporary squadron assignment, VS-56.*

When I finally got to Pensacola, the home of Naval Aviation, I was truly pumped. I passed my physical and got assigned a room in the old wooden WWII barracks: a nice room with a head at the end of the hall. I bought a Heath kit to build my own amplifier, got a turntable and a couple of speakers; after a while I had music when I could afford another LP album. Meanwhile I got to meet most of the Naval Academy football team. After graduating they came directly from the academy to play for the Goshawks, the Pensacola base football team. Roger Staubach was the quarterback from the previous academy season, future NFL great and played for the team. Soupy Campbell, the tight end, was in my dormitory and gave me lessons on how to make a frozen margarita straight from the academy recipe. He was in flight training whereas some of the other players were not.

Life was good; even though we weren't flying and were in ground school classroom studies, things couldn't be better.

After finishing ground school, I started driving out to Saufley Field to start flying the T-34. I was fortunate that I had over 200 hours of flight time in several different kinds of aircraft, which gave me an advantage going into flight training. I met several instructors spending their evenings at the bars on Pensacola beach. None of them were in my training flight but they knew I was a student, so they had some fun picking on me for not being in my room studying.

I didn't have my wings yet and that, along with the goal of finishing first in my class, was all that mattered. If you were first, they gave you what you wanted to fly. If not, you got what the Navy needed. My goal was a single seat jet, and anything less would be a major disappointment. Since this was before Vietnam really got hot, a jet seat was the hardest aircraft assignment to get, although each student finishing first at the end of training could also chose the multi-engine route or the helicopter route. I needed to be first in my graduating class to ensure I got my jet.

The training squadron, VT-1, consisted of four flights of about 30 student candidates each. This helped the squadron truly evaluate each student. To keep a consistency in training, students were checked by an instructor from a different flight to ensure quality of training. I was in flight four where all the instructors were Marine pilots. I planned very carefully what I had to do to finish number one. The Marines judged you on your appearance as well as your flying skills. Every day before I left my dorm, I ironed my pants and put three creases on the back of the shirt and two on the front, across each front pocket. I also had a full tie, not one of the clip-on types that the Marine instructors frowned on. They would pull on your tie and if it came off you were called a lazy "squid," their derogatory term for a Navy pilot. Every lunch time I went back to the dorm to re-iron my uniform. I was student-of-the week, an honor given to the highest-graded pilot in the week of his solo flight and first in my class as I left Saufley and the T-34 and headed for Meridian, Mississippi and the T-2 Buckeye Jet.

T2-B Buckeye photographed by the author. Note the gun attached under the wing.

CHAPTER THREE

Basic Jet Training

In January 1965 I joined VT-7 for jet training. The T-2B was my first jet. Sitting in the front seat with no propeller to obstruct the view, the nose quickly slanted down so all you saw was unfettered sky. What a treat. Quiet cockpit and it accelerated quickly: hard to believe I was finally flying a jet airplane. It reacted quickly and easily to all control inputs. I flew higher than I had ever flown. A clear sky, smooth air and everything on the ground seemed so small.

We learned basic aircraft maneuvering and acrobatics and improved our landing skills using a ground-based mirror system like that used on carriers. We were taught some basic instrument flying skills in preparation for advanced jet training. I was checked by an instructor from VT-9, our sister squadron, to ensure standards quality was being maintained throughout the wing. This instructor later became a squadron mate while I flew in Vietnam. His name was John McCain.

Later in 1965 I moved back to Pensacola and VT-4, again flying the T-2B. The mission now was to get training in air-to-air gunnery and to train to get our first carrier "trap," the term used for a carrier landing.

They hung a gun on each wing and had colored grease on the bullets so we could see who scored the most hits on a banner towed by another T-2B. We had to fly banner flights as well as the gunnery flights. Since we were not allowed to come up directly behind the banner to shoot (we would probably have shot down the banner aircraft) we never seemed to hit the banner. with the turn of your airplane and would determine the lead necessary to hit the target.

The author poses with MiG-17 Ace Nguyen Van Bay.

The plane had a gunsight that would track the target. The pipper, which was a lighted inverted V that the pilot was required to place on the target, would move around. This was deflection shooting, not really that great, especially for students; holding the bank of the airplane steady to try and keep the pipper from moving requiring a level of flying skill that we had not reached. I later met and talked to a MiG-17 ace from North Vietnam.

The day finally came when my class of four pilots was to finally "hit the boat," that is land aboard *USS Lexington*, CVA-16. We were to become "carrier pilots."

For several passes our hooks were up; the LSO (Landing Signal Officer) wanted to make sure we were capable of safe touch and go landings on the deck.

Then he radioed and instructed me to drop my hook. What a trip that was, until I trapped. I had never stopped so suddenly in my whole life. Even though I had locked my harness, I still slammed forward, and my knee-board slid all the way down my leg. When I recovered my senses, they gave me guidance to get clear of the landing area and go to the catapult ("the cat") so I could go again. Or so I thought. I was having trouble steering the plane and the flight deck boss told me I had a bad nose gear.

I was to go ashore and get a new aircraft. The cat shot went smoothly, but I was advised to not raise my gear in case it wouldn't retract properly. Since we were running out of daylight, I would not have time to return.

So, it was the following day that I completed my landings and started on my path to becoming a real carrier pilot. A true carrier pilot is one who has had a tour of duty aboard an aircraft carrier and survived.

CHAPTER FOUR

Advanced Jet Training

M y next stop was VT-23 in Kingsville Texas to begin training in the F9F Grumman Cougar jet. Grumman made extraordinarily strong, rugged airplanes, and ruggedness came with extra weight. The old jet engines weren't very powerful; it was affectionately known as the "lead sled." This was our advanced jet-training, the last stop before getting our wings.

I arrived with two other pilots, guys I had never met, so we were a huge class: three pilots. The first training was learning how to fly by instruments alone. I did very well in this area because I convinced myself that I wasn't flying; I just had to make these instruments do what they were supposed to do.

That philosophy has stayed with me ever since, and I really haven't ever had a problem with instrument flying. The base had a non-moving simulator that we used for practice before flying the real airplane. It was based on the old FJ Fury cockpit and had little micro switches I could feel; you only had to click them to a certain point and the airplane (simulator) flew simply fine. You could say

I was cheating, using the switches to fly the simulator, and you'd probably be right. I wasn't the first. There was no money in the Navy at that time to buy proper simulators.

The instructor was looking at a duplicate instrument panel next to the simulator. I had to climb a flight of wooden steps to get into the sim cockpit. For fun I would fly upside down. The instructor would question me about what I saw in the cockpit, and I would say it looked good. Eventually he came up the steps, which meant I could hear him coming. By the time he opened the canopy and looked in to see what I had, I had rolled it right side up. As he walked back down, I would roll it upside down again. I guess some would call me a smart ass, and that would probably be true, too, but it was fun.

The next phase was learning how to fly on the wing of another plane, a critical skill in military aviation. We started with a pair of two-seat F-9s with an instructor in the back seat and me up front. Holding a position a few feet off another plane's wing is not the easiest thing to do. Every time I lost position the instructor would take the stick and move us back into the proper position, return the controls to me and yell, "Stay in position, stupid." A highly effective method of teaching.

After several flights of learning how to stay in position straight and level, we practiced turns. We learned how to reduce power on the inside of the turn to maintain our position and to add power to remain in position on the outside. We learned crossovers, going from the right wing to the left wing.

We then moved on to four plane formations. As you add airplanes to the formation, especially with students, you get more moving planes—making it appear we were bouncing around. The lead pilot was supposed to fly a steady airspeed and steady altitude. Because he doesn't have to fly a position off another plane, he needs to fly smoothly to keep it steady. The number two pilot is trying hard to hold a position flying off a point on the lead aircraft. Being a student, he usually can't hold a rock-solid position, so he is moving a bit. Number three is now trying to stay with a moving airplane and gets a bit out of sync, so his movements are even bigger. By this time, poor number four is trying to stay with this bucking bronco, and he's producing even bigger movements. By the time we returned, the instructor had lost his voice from all the yelling. But it was fun for us, even if it wasn't for him.

In late January of 1966, we were doing gunnery flights in the single-seat F9. This aircraft at least had built in guns so it should have been more accurate than our T-2B. I was assigned the number

F9F Grumman Cougar.

four slot or "tail end Charlie" as it was sometimes known. We headed out to shoot. On the way, I began losing power, and the engine revolution speed (rpms) were cycling fast, then slow. At the same time, I lost the hydraulic power to the flight controls; fortunately, it had a backup manual flight control system. I informed the instructor that I had a problem. He asked if I thought I could get back to base. Of course, the only answer as a student was, "yes, I can."

Well, that was my plan. As I got closer to the base, everything seemed to get worse. The cockpit started to fill up with smoke, which I took as a bad sign. The Martin-Baker ejection seat was an old design, and the lowest altitude for a safe ejection was 2,500 hundred feet and flying a minimum of 120 knots airspeed.

I was coming to what was called "low key" or the last check point for a safe ejection before landing when the nose fell, pointing straight down, and I had no control over it or the plane. It was time to eject. As I pulled the ejection curtain that was at the top of the ejection seat and extended over the top of my helmet, I saw the fire warning light come on. A bit late I thought. Pulling the curtain was supposed to properly align one for the ejection sequence, but most of us still got a broken back (compression damage) or as we called it "A Martin-Baker back." Better a broken back than dead. Martin Baker I think was the first company to come up with a successful ejection seat. These seats saved many lives since this airplane was originally built without an ejection seat, which was typical for jets until late 1950s aircraft.

It was a very painful ride. I pulled at the rip cord. It didn't come out all the way (it wasn't designed to, I found out later). I was thinking, *OK now I am going to die!*

Then the 'chute opened, snapping me from a head down position to head up. I had a lot of pain in my left shoulder, but the snap of the chute opening made my shoulder feel better. Afterward, I was told by the doctor at my exam, that I probably had a dislocated shoulder.

As I descended, I could see the airplane on fire and heading for a chemical plant off the runway. I figured it would blow up south Texas, but it instead rolled left and headed for a car on the road. Fortunately, it missed the car. (I later found out that a mother and her young daughter were in it.)

The explosion of the plane hitting the ground was somewhat spectacular, like looking at a movie clip. I was alive, but my whole body hurt. The seat and I were the biggest parts to survive.

Finally, it came time to hit the boat again. The F9F Cougar jet had spoilers for turning, not ailerons. This meant reducing the lift on one wing caused the wing to drop and the plane to turn. This had the benefit of a trick way to lose altitude if you were high on the glide slope. To adjust quickly being high on the glide slope, one could move the stick right and left. This toggle caused enough loss of lift to get back on glide slope so qualifying with the "lead sled" was reasonably easy. Back to *USS Lexington*, CVA-16, to finish our advanced jet training.

PART II

Ready to Go

*Have enough courage to start and
enough heart to finish.*
Jessica N. S. Yourko

*The author, now a Naval Aviator, is sent to California to learn this war ma-
chine, the A4-E Skyhawk, one he will fly into combat. And his orders are to
join this squadron, one that paints a distinctive blue boomerang onto its tail.
He's almost ready, and soon he'll be flying it into North Vietnam.*

CHAPTER FIVE

The RAG: Final Preparation

It was 1966 and we were starting to bomb North Vietnam, where my new Squadron, VA-163, would soon be returning having been on some of the first missions in 1965. I just had to learn how to: fly the A-4, bomb a target, drop a nuclear bomb, refuel inflight and land on the carrier at night. Piece of cake.

As before in my training, every new stop along the way meant ground training where the Navy teaches you about the aircraft and its systems. Bombing techniques would be a new skill, nuclear school another new course, followed by what air to air refueling is all about and how this skill will be needed daily while deployed. Carrier landing at night was discussed; even though we had yet to do it, it was the hardest flying we would do.

There were two different models of the A-4: the C or "Charlie" model and the E or "Echo" model. The Echo had a different engine and wing configuration. The A-4 squadron to which you were assigned determined your training model. My squadron, VA-163, flew the Echo model; Larry Spear was my instructor. Larry had completed two tours as a VA-163 pilot. Larry wanted to make sure that I was good enough to join the squadron, and he was going to do everything in his power to make sure that I was well prepared. Since the A-4 was a single seat aircraft he would fly alongside of me or chase me from behind and instruct by radio if needed. On my first flight he briefed that we would fly to the mountains, where he wanted me to fly directly at the mountain and not climb until he ordered me to do so, and then pull the stick back as hard as I could. I trusted him so that was what I would do.

We went out and pre-flighted our airplanes. There was just one lesson that I learned that day that none of us had been taught in ground school: there was a delay between moving the throttle forward and getting power. I was quite surprised when I started to taxi; this delay caused me to over-compensate for the delay. I damn near got full power when it kicked in, and I had a bit of trouble turning out of the parking spot. I heard about that when I returned.

After we were airborne, he gave me directions to view and acquaint myself with our practice areas. Then he directed me into the mountains and had me fly directly at the mountain. It got bigger and bigger and I got worried and more worried; at the last possible second, he told me to head for the sky. I was climbing for about 30 seconds when he said look down at the mountain. I was amazed that I was so high above it. It was his way of introducing me to the performance of the A-4. A good lesson that I found useful the rest of my career flying the A-4.

Larry gave me more lessons in the capabilities of the plane, as well as formation flying, night flying and practice on the mirror when landing. Bombing practice began that involved rolling into a 45-degree dive from around 10,000 feet, looking through a bombsight and trying to get it on the target at a release altitude of around 4,000 feet and an airspeed of 450 knots (kts).

Each type of bomb that we carried had a different mil setting (an angular measurement) for the bombsight. The outside mil ring of the bombsight corresponded to the mil setting for the bomb, and you placed that ring on the target. As I was to fly down the bomb release angle, the sight picture would bring the caret (an inverted V, something like this ^) onto the target where I'd release the bomb. Wind also played a part in this scenario. If, for instance, it came from behind, it would push the dive path further ahead. I was to adjust by an offset—increasing the mil setting. If the wind came from either side, I'd need to use an offset left or right, which would allow the wind to push my dive-path to the correct release point. And in the same way, If I faced a headwind, I'd need to offset with a decrease in the mill setting. All these adjustments, with no real knowledge of what the wind was doing until I started the run, which mean I'd make the changes on the fly, so to speak.

As we began practicing this, we experienced misses by wide margins. But with experience, we became much better dive-bomb pilots. After my first combat cruise I had an average Circular Error Probable (CEP) of 28 feet. CEP is a measurement of all the artillery shells fired or bombs dropped, at a target.

The area that contains the 50 percentile of the hits defines the CEP. The second range is where the next 40 percent of ordnance would hit (2 x the first CEP) and the last is where the remaining shells or bombs would strike. To give this meaning, consider that a 500-pound MK 82 bomb with a delay fuse will create a hole 250 feet in diameter, and my CEP was 28 feet. If it were armed with a long-nosed fuse, the kill radius becomes 1000 feet.

We also had to qualify to drop a nuclear bomb before going to the next phase. (The Navy called it a "delivery," and we therefore became "nuclear delivery pilots.")

The practice bomb for this qualification was a 2000-pound concrete shape that simulated the aerodynamic characteristics of a big nuclear bomb. Our target was a big 1000-foot circle in the desert, and to qualify we were required to place that shape inside the circle. And our practice delivery was timed. We were required to place that shape in the target circle plus or minus 30 seconds from our target time.

My delivery flight took me out to sea about 200 miles, where I descended to 50 feet over the water and flew back toward the beach. There I picked up a defined route I had spent hours preplanning. I navigated using only a compass and clock over a vast stretch of uninhabited parts of Northern California and Nevada, flying fast and just 50 feet above the ground.

This was the Navy's tactic to avoid radar picking up speeding airplanes headed deep into enemy territory. My route that day was complex, and it included mountainous terrain. Using the clock on the cockpit window-bow in front of my face I ticked off the time for each leg, down to the second, with the map I had created for this flight on my kneeboard.

Depending on the maneuver I had planned and practiced, I was required to include the maneuver and the time the bomb would sail through the sky before it to hit the target on the precise assigned time.

For this flight, I planned an over-the-shoulder delivery, a toss accomplished by flying directly at the target, and then at the precise point I commenced a pull-up skyward, pulling a constant four Gs. The bomb released as I came up to a 120-degree angle and it flew skyward,

I continued pulling until I had completed about two-thirds of a loop and was flying away from the target. If it ever happened, hopefully I'd be far enough away before the bomb detonated.

This over-the-shoulder delivery would be used in many of the expected situations. Another version would be the same as the over-the-shoulder, but the angle the bomb would come off would be different—since we'd then be throwing it forward.

Again, we were to continue the pull-up, the four-G climb over the top of the partial loop and accelerate down the backside to get out of the bomb blast. Such a funny thought.

The next challenge was learning how to refuel in flight—in daylight and at night.

This was a challenging skill that would have to be performed even at night. My first event with this was indeed challenging. After putting the refueling probe in the basket, you had to push the hose

Two A-4 Skyhawks refueling. The bird in front, the tanker, has streamed a hose with a basket on the end, and the second airplane has pushed its probe into that. The tarker pumps fuel to the plane that has "plugged in."

several feet into the buddy store (name of the refueling unit) before fuel could be transferred. I was the last student to practice this skill and after a few tries I got hooked up to the hose, but as I tried to push it forward, the hose didn't retract; it started folding into a sinusoidal curve under the pressure of being pushed toward the buddy store and not retracting into the unit and then it burst showering my canopy with fuel. Fuel flowed into the engine air intake and set the fuel on fire. I now had a fireball around my cockpit; my aircraft was accelerating, taking me under the refueling tanker, even though I had pulled my throttle to idle.

The other students yelled at me to eject but the instructor told me to extend the speed brakes. That worked and my aircraft dropped back, but my probe was so bent that when I got disconnected, the basket ripped off and was stuck on my bent probe. Kind of crazy. The instructor gave me s**t for screwing up. He later joined my squadron as a replacement pilot in 67 and still gave me s**t. Just another day as a Naval aviator. I never had that problem again, so why it didn't retract, I never knew.

The A-4 with "my basket" stuck on its bent refueling probe. It looks worse than it was, and the probe was quickly changed for a straight one.

The last challenge was our carrier landings. This time it would include night landings. Our practice was held at night on a normal runway, with the LSO who would also be our LSO on the boat. On about the third night I had a problem that, while dangerous, gave me practice in controlling a problem I would encounter in combat. As I was making my first takeoff that night when I got to the normal rotate speed the nose wouldn't come up. As the speed increased the aircraft suddenly rotated to an ever-increasing nose high position. I am a big user of the trim button and immediately put nose down trim, to stabilize the pitch and speed. I had a bit of trouble leveling off and then turning to go downwind in the pattern, but everything was under control, or so I thought. I was flying a wide pattern, but I got back around to align and make a good approach. We were doing touch-and-go landings and after touchdown I pulled the stick back to rotate but the nose didn't move.

As speed increased it quickly rotated and kept increasing the nose up pitch and again, I ended up in a wide pattern. As I got on final approach the LSO told me to tighten up my pattern and I responded, "Aye aye, sir!" a proper Navy response.

Trying to rotate resulted in the same problem of the nose not responding and then over responding. I was getting pissed at myself for not flying better. To keep a tighter pattern, I rolled in a steep bank angle, and suddenly, the aircraft nose fell through and I was looking at the ground rushing up. I immediately rolled wings level and the nose came back up. I reported to the LSO that I had a flight control problem; after the landing I taxied to the ramp and requested another aircraft. I finished the hop without any further problems.

When I reported in the next morning the maintenance chief came up to me and asked if I was the one who wrote up the broken airplane. I admitted that I was, and he showed me pictures of what went wrong.

When they first went to the airplane and started it up to check the flight controls the maintenance sailor reported that the controls felt fine in the cockpit. The chief responded that might be true, but the elevator (the flight control that controls the pitch of the airplane) wasn't moving. They found that a pin had not been secured properly and disconnected the push rod from the elevator control horns; I had no elevator control. From that night forward, day or night, after starting up, I kept my canopy open so I could watch the elevator move in the cockpit mirrors.

After all that had happened, I was looking forward to getting to the boat and away from these planes trying to kill me. The boat we were assigned for qualification traps was USS Bennington, CVA-

20 launched in 1944. She had the first hydraulic catapults, which give a rough ride. It hurts!

The daylight landings went well; the night ones were exciting, scary, raising the heart rate for sure. All black, no horizon to help in knowing whether you were upside down, or right side up, which is the preferable option. You can't see the ship, just a few lights for the landing area, along with the ball for the glide scope.

The flying aboard Bennington was extensive. I got in two touch-and-goes, 18 day-traps and eight arrested landings at night. My logbook shows I was aboard three days. It also shows that I went back two days later to make two more day-traps and a night arrested landing—but I don't recall this, and wonder if it is a mistake. My logbook shows nothing about how I got back to the ship to do that. But the way we remember things is funny; perhaps it did happen and I just no longer recall.

Nevertheless, when I returned to Lemoore, I was fully qualified to fly an A-4 onto and off a ship. It was time to join my squadron which was now off the coast of North Vietnam.

CHAPTER SIX

Finally, Off to Combat

It was a bit like the movie Trains, Planes, and Automobiles. Before leaving I first had to find a place to store my car. I found a gas station in Hanford, California that had a building in which to store it. I jacked it up and put it on blocks to protect the tires. I had to pay monthly storage fees, but I don't remember what the cost was. I then needed to store all my other belongings in a storage room that the Navy provided in the Bachelor Officers Quarters (BOQ).

Getting out to Yankee Station was not an easy thing to do. I had a friend drive me to the airport in Fresno to catch a flight to San Francisco. I then took a bus to Travis Air Force base, where in the early morning I boarded a charter airliner for a flight to Clark Air Force base in the Philippines.

Once at Clark I had to catch another bus to Subic Bay, the main Navy base. It happens it was a local Filipino bus which didn't have much room; it was a bit beat up and didn't have a lot of power. I wasn't sure it could climb some of the small mountains between Clark and Subic Bay. It did make it to Olongapo City which allowed me to walk to the base.

After reporting to Subic Bay, they told me there was no way to get to the *USS Oriskany* (CVA-34) except by oiler, which would take about a week.

An interesting way to get to war. I boarded an oiler. I think it was *USS Caliente* AO-53. I'm not sure that is the correct ship, but I was treated well.

I had no duties, and I was bored. We supplied fuel oil to several ships on the way to *Oriskany*.

The author's photo is of a refueling process in rather heavy seas. An aircraft carrier needs fuel for its own power, as well as fuel for its aircraft.

When we arrived alongside *Oriskany*, she was launching airplanes, so the oiler was now matching the speed of *Oriskany*, about 20 knots, as the hoses were pulled across the turbulent sea.

A bosun's chair, a steel cage, really, was rigged, and I rode it across the churning sea with my seabag in my lap. It was late July of 1966 and I had just turned 24 years old. There I was floating over a pitching sea wondering if I would be taking a dunking. The noise of jets being catapulted drowned out the yells of the sailors as I was pulled me closer and closer to my new home. I think they would have liked to see me dunked, but they worried about getting into trouble. If the cable broke, I wouldn't survive that but then what did I care. I wasn't sure I would survive the war either.

I caught up with my squadron, VA-163, the "Saints" presently assigned to USS *Oriskany*, CVA-34, "The Mighty O" and my new home. I had lived aboard a ship as a midshipman, but this was the real thing. I was by now a Lieutenant Junior Grade (LTJG), but to my shipmates I was a "nugget," a new guy. The term came from the fact that most of the new guys were Navy Ensigns and wore a single gold bar on their uniforms.

It really didn't matter what your rank was. If you hadn't had an active-duty cruise, you were a "nugget." The squadron was presently flying combat missions over North Vietnam; if you hadn't flown combat before, you were more of a "nugget-nugget" or in mathematical terms, Nugget^2.

Since I was a junior officer, I was assigned to a junior officer's (JO) bunkroom. This was a large room that had about ten bunk-beds, storage closets and a bathroom—in nautical terms, a head.

My new quarters, this bunk room, was on the O-2 level, which was just below the flight deck. It had one advantage: it was one of the few spaces on the *Oriskany* that was air conditioned. Since I had arrived late, all the lower bunks were taken so I grabbed a top bunk. Later I would find out why the top bunks were all empty.

As a new guy, I was given a mandatory tour of the ship. They didn't provide you with a nicely colored brochure showing you where you were or where the wardroom was (for meals and relaxation) or where the ready room was to go to work. Even though this was an old WWII type of carrier, exceedingly small compared to the giants of today, it was still the biggest ship I had ever been on and getting lost was quite easy. For those who have never been on a US Navy warship, you might think the old hunk of iron is just that: a hunk of dead iron floating on the sea. You would be wrong.

What has always amazed me was how alive the ship was. The nerves (electrical cabling) of the ship passed through every compartment (room), passageway (hall) and every conceivable nook and cranny, making the ship hum. As you progressed lower into the bowels of the ship, the noise of machinery driving and steering the iron monster seemed to sound like a grumbling stomach.

As you got to the higher levels of the ship, you heard the arresting cable sliding back across the flight deck as it released the aircraft from its grip. It sounded like old bones creaking. If they were launching aircraft, you heard the boom of the catapult as it slammed against the bow of the ship and threw aircraft into the air. It was as if the old monster were belching. Yes, an active naval ship is alive. You only need visit it while it is on active duty and then again after it has been retired to know the difference.

This was my new home and would be my home on and off until January of 1968. After reporting into the squadron and getting the ship's tour, I was ready to try my new bed. It had been a long day, and it didn't take but a few seconds before I was sleeping like the proverbial baby. I'm not sure how long I had been asleep, but suddenly, I felt water dripping on me. As I awoke, I could tell it wasn't dripping, it was more like rain. In fact, from all I could tell in the darkened room, it was raining throughout the whole compartment. From the laughter of my roommates, this was a common thing. When it rained topside (outside) it rained in through our ceiling as the roof, the steel deck below the wood flight deck, had long since been rusted through. That's why none of the top bunks were taken.

That wasn't the only problem. I had left my new brown shoes (aviators wore brown shoes with a khaki uniform while regular navy ship officers wore black shoes) on the deck (floor). They were nowhere to be seen until one of my roommates mentioned he saw them floating over near the head. From that time on those shoes squeaked; being a bit stubborn, I refused to buy new ones

The next morning, I went among my new roommates until I found one junior to me using a lower bunk and I employed my rank to summarily throw him out. At least I had a bunk for a roof and from then on, I put my shoes in my closet. First problem solved.

When you join a squadron as a "nugget" you don't have a nickname which will normally be your radio call sign. You don't get the chance to pick your nickname. After a short time, someone will pick one for you. After a couple of weeks, our operations officer, LCDR Clem Morrisette, gave me my official "Saint" nickname, "Animal." I was quite surprised because I was known as "Animal" (being a wrestler) during my college years, and I didn't mind it. Had anyone learned that I liked it, it would have been changed, so I kept my mouth shut. (Something my friends would find funny)

Even though we had wings and we flew daily, aviators also had other squadron duties. The Skipper summoned the new guy to his stateroom so he could get to know him better, laid down his rules and then told you what your extracurricular duties were.

I was now the "Materiel Officer," responsible for keeping the squadron fully supplied with shoes, toilet paper, fuel, engine parts, helmets and just about anything you can think of that is needed to keep a combat squadron of A-4s flying. I also had to keep track of the money spent so that we wouldn't run out of money before the next fiscal year. Not the most glamorous job but one that gives a-good insight into how things get done. Navy Chiefs are equivalent to senior sergeants in the other armed forces and they made sure that we young "nuggets" didn't screw up the whole Navy. I was blessed with a great Chief so all I had to do to learn was listen. I thank God for Navy Chiefs!

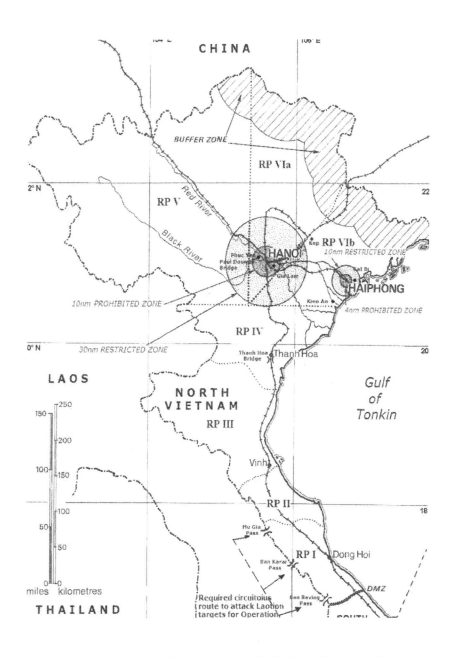

This Map shows how North Vietnam was divided into Route Packs numbered as RP I, RP II, RP III, RP IV, RP V, RP VIa and RP VIb. The US Air Force was initially assigned RP I, RP V and RP VIa, and the remaining packs were the responsibility of the US Navy.

CHAPTER SEVEN

Rules of the War: 1966

The map on page 50 shows how North Vietnam was initially divided into areas of responsibility, a move designed to keep inter-
service rivalries in check. The Navy would limit its air war in this
scheme to Route Package II, part of the panhandle below Vinh; RP
III, which was Vinh and north of there; RP IV, a region in which the
Than Hoa Bridge (a very tough target) was located; and RP VIb, a
region between Hanoi and Haiphong (with restricted zones surrounding both of those key cities).

Our primary mission was to interdict (stop) supplies reaching
South Vietnam. The restricted areas around Hanoi and Haiphong
prohibited us from attacking there unless authorized by Washington. Another restriction was we couldn't drop on a gun emplacement unless it was shooting at us. If a gun emplacement or missile

site were under construction, we were not allowed to drop on it. (These hit us hard in '67)

At the start of 1965, the primary Navy mission was to provide close air support to the ground troops. The station off the coast was called "Dixie Station." When the missions in the north first started in mid-1965, a carrier was moved north to a new station called "Yankee Station." With the buildup in South Vietnam of new ground air bases and expanding missions in the North, a second carrier was moved to "Yankee Station." One carrier adopted a flight schedule of midnight to noon and the other to noon to midnight. That way we had airplanes over North Vietnam all day, every day. A third carrier was brought in to start at Dixie and as relief for one of the carriers at Yankee to provide R&R for the troops.

On occasion Washington would decide to order a big strike on some target. This usually involved both carriers hitting the same target one after the other. That meant flying all our A-4s from both A-4 squadrons on each ship: 20 aircraft each time on target. The former schedule resumed until the next big strike. Though we lost aircraft to ground fire, the overall threat was less than we would experience in '67.

CHAPTER EIGHT

Air Wing 16

Air Wing 16 assigned to *Oriskany* consisted of two F-8 fighter squadrons, VF-111 and VF-162 each with 12 "Crusaders"; two A-4 squadrons VA-163 and VA-164 (the world-famous Ghost Riders) each with 12 "Skyhawks;" and an A-1 squadron VA-152 with 12 "Spads. "

The airwing also included specialized aircraft such as a recon-photo F-8, a radar plane ("Queer Spad"), which was an A-1 with four crew members aboard and a radar antenna underneath, or a "Willie Fudd," an E-1 Tracer with a big radar dome on top of the wing; several helicopters, a COD (carrier onboard delivery); and a Douglas A-3 "Skywarrior" for airborne refueling.

That made for a crowded deck on a small carrier; many planes were kept below on the hangar bay. Each fighter and attack squadron had about 14 pilots; the pilot complement for the other squadron detachments was dictated by its mission.

This E-1 (Willy Fudd) is about to launch. Photo by the author.

The F-8 Crusader snatching a wire in this photo belongs to one of the two fighter squadrons aboard Oriskany.

PART III

First Combat

Tough times never last, but tough people do.
Robert H. Schuller

On centerline and grabbing a three-wire. Ready for Southeast Asia.

CHAPTER NINE

Our Missions in '66

In 1966 most of our flying was recce (reconnaissance) missions, where we looked for moving equipment such as trucks, barges and trains, anything that could move materiel and men to South Vietnam. We would fly as a two-man section, the leader down at a lower altitude so he could spot the equipment and the wingman up high so he could protect the leader, call out anyone shooting and be in a position to immediately roll in on the target.

In the daylight hours we were highly effective in stopping traffic. Night was a different story. The A-4 was never designed for a night mission. If you had the instrument lights on, they reflected off the canopy so that you couldn't see outside very well; at the lowest light setting in the bombsight, you couldn't see the target through the bombsight.

To help us during the night missions, we used flares. Old, practice-bomb racks were modified to carry three flares; each pilot had three flares and then usually five, 500-pound bombs as well as a

400-gallon, centerline, fuel tank. We had a great deal of trouble with the flares igniting while still in the bomb rack, a problem that would cause an even bigger problem later in the cruise.

We dropped the flares at an altitude five to six thousand feet. The flares had a timer. They would freefall for ten seconds before a chute opened; ten seconds after the chute opened, they would light up. They were very bright and illuminated the area like daylight. We rolled in at about 10,000 feet, dove below the flare and dropped our bombs. Since we couldn't use our bombsight or our flight instruments, we were not always that accurate. But if the US Air Force bombed at night so did the Navy. I know it's hard to believe, but we were in competition with the US Air Force, as much as we were with the North Vietnamese.

This wasn't the only competition taking place. A large board on the front of our ready room kept track of each pilot's landing grade. The Landing Signal Officer (LSO) graded every approach made to the ship even if the approach resulted in a wave off (do not attempt a landing), a bolter (a touchdown but missed wire) or a trap (landing catching a wire). The grades were given a color, and these were prominently displayed on the board for all to see. Our squadron's color was blue, so a blue color signified an "OK" grade. If you got an "OK" underlined grade they marked the blue with an underline. Not many of those were ever given but were counted as a "10." From there you went down to zero which was a "Cut" (Red color) or dangerous approach.

No secrets about one's ability to land on the carrier. The pilot with the best landing results (highest number) during a line tour (combat time) won the pot of money collected from pilots who made various mistakes: returning to the wrong ship or not putting the hook down before calling the ball. I did not win a pot in 1966. Peer pressure encouraged me to do better, and I did improve.

I was learning how to become a better Navy Officer and a better pilot. VA-163's nickname was the Saints and the radio call sign was "old salt," a proper Navy term. The Saints were one of the top naval aviation squadrons and I considered myself fortunate to be a Saint and learn my craft from my squadron mates.

CHAPTER TEN

On the Line

On my first mission, I flew with an experienced pilot, Lieutenant (LT) Bob Hafford, who was on his second tour. Bob was a sharp pilot and it was very brave to take on a "nugget" and attempt to teach him how to survive a combat mission and hit the target.

After the cat shot, we climbed to altitude and headed toward the shore of North Vietnam. In our jargon, we called it heading for the beach. Once we were over land, we were "feet dry." Likewise, when we crossed the beach outbound and were heading back out to sea, we were "feet wet."

On this, my first mission, we were going after a fuel supply dump, close to the port city of Haiphong.

Bob briefed that we would start south of our intended target near the city of Vinh, then fly northward along the coast toward our target. As we got closer to shore Bob commanded that we arm our weapon systems, and I replied that I was now armed.

It was at this moment I realized that this was for real. I would be dropping actual weapons, 500-pound bombs, not practice bombs. And I could possibly kill someone or seriously destroy property of another country.

Flying along the coast gave me many mixed feelings of what we were about to do. It was a beautiful, bright blue sky, and the coastline had some very nice and enticing beaches. The green-covered hills were shaped differently than any mountains I had ever seen before. It looked very peaceful until we began our attack; we had reached our target.

Then fireballs came up toward us, exploding in big white puffs. Bob commented that these were 37mm guns now shooting at us.

Bob found our target, and we both scored good hits; a big fireball confirmed fuel was indeed there.

However, by some oversight, both of us failed to turn on our missile warning system. As soon as we did, they started pinging loudly, indicating that missile-control radar was tracking us. We were under threat of a missile launch. I didn't get to see much of that area of Vietnam as we hurriedly left, heading south of Haiphong where there were fewer problems with guns and missiles.

It was beautiful countryside to view—if they weren't shooting at you.

Finally, we were feet wet and headed home. This was my first combat mission, and the first thing that truly captured my attention wasn't getting shot at but rather a low fuel-gauge reading of 500 pounds as I "called the ball" (the landing guide). During all my training in the A-4 Skyhawk when we reached 1,000 pounds of fuel remaining, we landed. So, from my previous experience I was sure I was close to a flame-out: if you run out of fuel, the flame powering the engine quits. That's pretty basic.

The low fuel reading was giving me fits, and I didn't feel comfortable. However, as a nugget I knew to keep quiet. As I got more familiar with operating around the carrier, I realized that 500 pounds of fuel would give me a normal first approach, if you were waved off or missed a wire, you would have about 250 pounds of fuel to get to the tanker for more fuel. I later could get an approach in, if there were no other traffic in the pattern, with 300 pounds of fuel remaining.

A little history: while I was enroute to join VA-163, the squadron's current Skipper was hit by flak. He lost the lower part of his right arm, but he was able to fly to feet wet and eject. He was rescued and of course hospitalized.

The executive officer then became the Skipper and a new executive officer arrived. He didn't have to catch an oiler as I did; he had the rank of Commander (Lieutenant Colonel in the Army).

Since we were both new to the squadron I was assigned as his permanent wingman. I was now on the wing of CDR Bryan "Magnolia" Compton, a very experienced pilot and extremely aggressive. He demanded performance, and if I missed with my bomb, he said that I was wasting taxpayer money and that I better get better.

The only acceptable response was "Aye aye, Sir," and hope I could improve. If I didn't, I wasn't sure where the Navy might send me. As it worked out, we made a good team, he had confidence he would survive, so that meant that I would as well.

CHAPTER ELEVEN

First R&R

The only places to go were the city of Olongapo which I didn't care for, the black shoe, (Ship Officer nickname) Subic Bay Officers' club which was very elegant, or the Cubi Point Officers' club a.k.a., the Brown Shoe club (pilots). It was a left-over, old concrete structure from WWII; it had a huge picture window overlooking the runway. We witnessed some exciting stuff from up there—and with a drink in our hand. We'd laugh at the accidents; happy it wasn't us causing them. To enter the club, you had to have a coat and tie on, or for a buck you could rent a Barong Tagalog, a formal Filipino dress shirt made from plants. We all paid the buck, took off the shirt we had on and put on the one they handed us. It worked for me.

The ceiling was made with woven mats. When a fight started, you could crawl up there and jump down on someone or hit them over the head with whatever was in your hand. It was amazing the ceiling didn't catch fire when we lit "after burners." To do this, we'd fill our mouth with lighter fluid, then blow it out at a lit cigarette-lighter. Boy did it light up— a human flame-thrower. Yes, boys will be boys.

We also had some good games to play to keep us entertained. The first was night cat shots. A simple game.

We'd put a pilot in a chair, put a blinder over his eyes, open the door, four guys would pick up his chair and we'd throw him into the jungle. Great fun.

Only one got lost in the jungle; we had to get a couple indigenous Filipinos, men who understood the jungles, to go look for him. These were the same guys we had to hide from in our jungle evasion course. They always found us, so they easily found our lost catapult victim.

The other game was simple as well. We'd put a couple of tables together, lather them down with beer, get some toilet paper for the landing cable, run and jump sliding along the table and try to catch the cable with our foot. If the cable broke, too bad.

We modified this for more fun by putting blinders on the players so they could do night landings. If he got too low, he just hit his head—which in this game meant you were dead. Drinking plenty of alcohol made these antics seem wonderfully fun.

We enjoyed drinking the local San Miguel beer, and one of the hot dogs available at the bar was always a treat. We believed that the American beers that had been shipped from the States had a bit of formaldehyde in them to prevent the beer from spoiling, so we thought they tasted terrible.

The concrete rooms in the BOQ had jalousie-style windows that cranked open but did not shut very well, so we had various jungle creatures that occupied the rooms with us.

The squadron had some of the experienced pilots that were to do some cross-deck operations with the British ship HMS Hermes. This gave our pilots experience with landings and catapults on foreign ships. while the Brits then did the same, flying onto and off of the Mighty O. While I was scheduled to fly out to the ship and be aboard to witness this operation, I had a problem of no oil pressure indicated for my engine at start up. I was therefore delayed and missed the show.

CHAPTER TWELVE

Second On Line Period

Eventually all good things come to an end. As I mentioned, my airplane had an oil pressure gauge that was fluctuating in the airplane I was to fly from Cubi. A mechanic decided it was OK for me to launch, so after a delay, I was headed back to the Mighty O, our ship without shower-water, without milk, and with only bug-juice to drink, interesting food and the occasional saltwater shower. It was back to 12-hour flight operations, a day hop and one at night.

I was making many carrier landings and getting in plenty of bombing experience, so I was improving in both skill areas.

And I was still flying on Magnolia's wing, working to improve, trying to stop him from telling me that I was wasting taxpayer money.

In September, an F-8 saw a moving train, in broad daylight no less, and put a heat-seeking Sidewinder missile in the engine to stop it. As Magnolia and I were next on the schedule, we quickly were launched with other A-4s. All In all, there were eight of us.

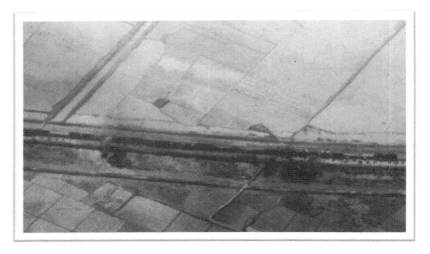

*The author's photo of the train stopped by an F-8 pilot's
heat-seeking missile, then bombed by the author and other A-4s.*

We had two F-8s airborne with us for MiG cover.

The train was stuck between the cities of Nam Dinh and Ninh Binh. Both cities had guns, a 57mm gun in Ninh Binh and an 85mm in Nam Binh. I learned to tell the difference. The 57 comes up and explodes in black, the 85 explodes with a big red ball then goes black. They weren't close to us, so dropping on the train was easy work.

Eventually we were warned—I think it was Big Sky, the call-sign of one of the aircraft electronically monitoring enemy activity—that there were MiG's on the way. But that didn't stop us.

However, unknown to me at the time, one of the MiG's was being flown by Nguyen Van Bay, the future MiG-17 Ace whom I would meet years later.

He shot down one of the F-8s and his wingman caused damage to the other.

Since we were just about out of bombs, we dropped what was left and headed for the water.

CHAPTER THIRTEEN

Second R&R

At the end of September, we were released for another break. With longer leave we left the line for Sasebo, Japan. From there it was on to Hong Kong.

On the way we encountered a bad storm, during which we received a message that a civilian freighter was in trouble. *Oriskany* launched her helicopter and rescued the crew. This was a great accomplishment for these pilots and crew, and in Hong Kong they received a nice trophy, an acknowledgement of their heroism by the grateful freighter's corporation.

On our way, as we entered the Sea of Japan, two changes took place. Each A-4 was loaded with a nuclear weapon, checked by the pilot to ensure it could be armed; if ordered we could launch against targets assigned to each pilot.

The other change was that F-8s stood ready for launch, two hooked to the catapult. It was tradition that the Russians would overfly the carrier as it entered the Sea of Japan. The F-8s were to intercept the aircraft before it got to the ship, then escort it as it flew over the ship. As expected, the call came to launch the F-8s.

This photo and the one below, shot by the author, is the Soviet "Bear" bomber, that he intercepted as it headed toward Oriskany. He was directed to it by radar operators. "A very cool experience," in his words.

I was in the duty A-4 tanker and would launch after the F8s and be available to give them fuel on returning. My other job was to get a picture of the Russian escorted by the F-8 with the ship in the background. I couldn't use my personal camera, I had to use an official, Navy camera. Both F-8s went down broken; I was launched and given vectors to intercept the inbound Russian "Bear," which I did.

After the second picture, however, the camera jammed. Fortunately, I got these, or I would have been in trouble with the Skipper of the ship, CAG (Commander of the Air Group) and of course my own Skipper Commander (CDR) Caldwell.

Both Japan and Hong Kong were exciting and fun spots. No fighting ashore but plenty of good food, milk and great ice cream. In Japan, these were not expensive (a favorable exchange rate meant more Japanese Yen for our dollar).

Watches, stereo equipment and cameras were within the buying range of a junior Naval officer. Hong Kong was a bit more expensive since they used the English pound for currency. Since we were on a smaller carrier, we could get in close to the city, so it was a short trip ashore. We rented a suite for the squadron and called it "admin ashore." It was loaded with booze and became a place to relax after shopping, eating and drinking, which is a major pasttime for those who get shot at daily.

Hong Kong was one of the only free-trade cities in the world. And it was the most interesting and exciting city I had ever been to. The city was full of exotic, beautiful women.

Citizens of many nations lived there; excellent restaurants served food from all these different countries, and the food was delicious, and if not, the restaurant wouldn't make it in such demanding city.

By chance I had shore patrol duty the first night in Hong Kong. This was a learning experience I repeated on the first night each time we went there. As shore patrol, we went in the bars that normally served Navy personnel.

The noticeably big sailors I had with me, would go through the bar looking for anyone too drunk, anyone sleeping or the occasional guy wanting to fight over a woman.

While they cruised the bar, I sat with the lady of the house who ran things. They were happy to have us there; it was protection for them. We would talk over some hot tea.

The next night if I happened to visit the bar, the lady of the house made sure I had the best table for the floor show, the best-looking lady to sit at the table with me and was served the good liquor.

I had to pay of course but it was a nice treat.

Later that same evening, I bought supper for my guys. We wanted Italian and entered a restaurant where we were greeted by a gentleman that I presumed to be the manger.

He escorted us to our table, used fresh garlic to wipe the inside of the wood bowl in which he made our salad, and it was a delicious dinner.

The next year I remembered where the restaurant was and took the guys there for dinner. As we entered this same gentleman came running up to me, gave me a big hug, escorted us to a private area and treated us to dinner.

I didn't understand this generosity. He explained that I was his first ever customer. He had had a very successful year, and he attributed it to me, his good luck charm. He was the owner!

I felt truly honored. Such a nice, hard-working person.

CHAPTER FOURTEEN

Back on the Line

It was now the first of October. We headed back to Yankee Station, and October brought the monsoon season to North Vietnam. We had to deal with heavy rain, heavier than I had ever encountered.

Our aircraft incurred major damage to their radomes, the fiberglass covers for the radars at the nose of the airplane. We solved this problem by covering the nose with layers of bomb tape, today now known as duct tape.

This tape was brown in color instead of silver and was used to tape the bomb arming wire to the bomb. It was also used to temporarily repair holes in the plane.

The tape ablated away. (Ablated is a scientific term used to describe a surface to be sacrificed. The protection for the space capsules had a coating that ablated, protecting the surface of the capsule). Our tape was sacrificed in the heavy rain, thus protecting the radomes.

Eventually the Navy used a rubber coating to keep the radome from getting damaged.

The other big problem of the monsoon season was the disruption to the flight schedule. Every flight became a weather-checker throughout the North. Because of this weather, we sometimes returned with our ordnance. And sometimes we had to release at secondary targets.

This continued until a fateful day—October 26, 1966.

CHAPTER FIFTEEN

Fire, Fire!

Man living on a ship is centuries old, yet it is completely different from living on land. If you live on land and your home catches fire, you can escape outside and safely watch or fight the fire. If a ship catches fire, there was no place to escape the fire; if you don't fight the fire, you soon might be swimming in the open sea, not necessarily a safe place.

On October 26, 1966, *Oriskany* had the first catastrophic carrier fire since WWII.

We were the midnight-to-noon carrier, and I had briefed at 2200 hours for the midnight launch. Off we went into a dark night with bad weather in the target areas. My next mission was delayed and then canceled finally about 0600. I went to my quarters in the upper (second deck) JO (Junior Officer) bunk room located just under the flight deck and just forward of mid-ship. This JO bunk room is different from the one located forward. I went to sleep quickly. The next thing I remember is hearing a sailor's voice on the 1MC stating, "This is a drill. This is a drill. Fire. Fire. Fire forward starboard side ...."

I rolled over and was trying to go back to sleep. LTJG "Scotty" Wilkens, the squadron air intelligence officer, came in with the door closing with a loud bang, yelling that we were on fire.

Oriskany burns. This was the first major fire on a US Navy ship since the Second World War—devastating.

The smoke that followed him meant that we really had a fire. There were about eight of us in the room and we calmly dressed and discussed our options. We decided to try and crawl out the back way and I suggested that we wet towels to wrap around our nose and mouth. While I was in the head (Navy for lavatory) wetting my towel, I looked at all the steel around me and knew that I couldn't break my way out. We left crawling along in the dark, each holding on to the belt of the man in front. We made it to the gun tub on the side of the ship that was upwind of the fire and clear of smoke.

Being on board a ship in trouble is different from most other situations. Your ship is your floating home; if she goes under, so do you. So, all on board, regardless of rank will work together to

save her. The fire resulted from the inadvertent storage of an activated flare in a munitions locker. The fire killed 44 pilots and seamen and another 156 were injured.

Scotty Wilkins. Photo by the author.

The following are the recollections of several of my squadron
mates as well as LTJG Tony Chibbaro, a ship's company officer:

LTJG, Chibbaro was asleep in his bunk in the forward 01 Junior
Officer's bunkroom. Tired from completing a 12-hour shift, he
rolled over in bed. ENS "Chico" Tardio my squadron mate pulled
the curtain to his bunk and said, "Tony, it's really bad. You have to
get up!"

He left Tony in bed, left the bunkroom and ran aft, unknow-
ingly in the direction of the fire. He did not survive. Chibbaro
dressed and as he left the room another officer directed him forward into the forecastle. As he climbed through the hatch an explosion blew him through the hatch and onto the flight deck.

My squadron mate, LT "Moose" Lundy, was taxiing, preparing for a mission, when he noticed smoke coming from the starboard side, forward of the island.

The Air Boss shut down the flight deck; Moose saw LTJG Chuck Nelson, a pilot from VA-164, stagger toward the plane, retching from the effects of the smoke.

ENS "Ralph" Bisz another squadron mate, found his way onto the deck with singed hair from a close encounter with the flames.

Bombs were pushed over the side as the fire raged.

AT3 Ed Copher a squadron mate was in his rack, putting on his shoes, when he heard the announcement of the fire in the forward hangar bay. His bunkroom was one deck down from the rear of the flight deck, near the starboard side fantail; the smoke quickly became so thick that he could not see to tie his shoes. He moved to the hangar bay, and realized that the overhead saltwater, sprinkler system had been activated. He saw that the flare locker was on fire, and many of the crew had started to move planes (some of which were on fire) onto the elevators. Several of the officers, whose bunkrooms were near the fire, had died in the fire and were being evacuated on the elevator and the catwalks. Some of the crew assisting in the recovery were overcome by smoke, revived and returned to assist in recovery of the deceased.

While moving one of the planes, an ejection seat in a plane near Ed exploded and drove the seat halfway through the canopy of the plane. This caused him to have flashbacks for the next two to three years until he managed to resolve the stress on his own.

Clean air can be found on the flight deck.

LCDR. Marv Reynolds' room was near the fire. His roommate was faster getting dressed in response to the emergency and was the first to leave the room. He left the room turning left in the passageway right into the fire and died. Marv closed the door and tried to use towels around the door to prevent the smoke from entering the room, but he was not successful. The wall caught fire, and he used the water from his sink to control it. His room filled with smoke; he opened a porthole to get air and got his head through it. The "Angel" helicopter was on station on the starboard side of the ship, its normal station to cover the launch that was scheduled at the same time the fire started. The pilots of the helicopter saw Marv staring at them from his porthole.

Using hand signals, Marv got the crew to understand that he needed a fire hose. Members of the crew on the deck swung a fire-hose to him; he spent the next three hours fighting the fire in his room. After the ship was repaired, per Navy existing regulations, the porthole was welded closed. It was to Marv's good fortune that someone did not follow the regulations when the ship was built during WWII.

After 14 hours of midnight flight operations, AE-3 Hubert Cook, of my squadron, had fallen asleep in the Flight Deck Mainte-nance shack. He was awakened by Chief Bagwell to go service an A-4 awaiting clearance to launch. After he replaced a fuse and as-sisted loading some bombs on aircraft being readied for missions, he heard a loud boom that came from forward of the island and

then dark smoke started pouring aft over the flight deck. The angle elevator brought up an A-4 that was heavily charred and blistered.

A mix of sailors lent their strength pushing the damaged jet off the elevator and chaining it in place. Sailor Cook was re-tasked to firefighting for a while and then joined an officer on a search-and-rescue mission in the forward quarters area, without much success. He returned to the flight deck and saw the result of effective disaster triage: those who were alive were receiving treatment; those who weren't were covered with sheets or blankets.

LTJG Dave Carey, a squadron mate, was in his quarters on the port side of the ship. He initially ignored the alarm but saw smoke leaking into his room. He dressed in his flight suit and boots and stepped into a passageway that was so full of smoke as to have zero visibility. He felt his way aft along the bulkheads and eventually reached the Administrative Office, which had an air conditioner installed and was disconnected from the ventilation system.

Several junior enlisted seamen were in the office and the air was clear of smoke. The ship's communications were down. They attempted to go farther aft but could not make it through the smoke. They retreated to the Admin Office and had to lie on the floor to get some breathable air. One of Dave's academy classmates, Jim Nunn, arrived in scuba gear with several gas masks as well.

Dave and Jim sent the sailors on their way with the face masks and instructions as to how to find good air and then the two officers continued to search for survivors in the officer quarters area. But their efforts were to no avail. They came up to the flight deck and found many members of their squadron.

Later as night began to fall and we were steaming toward the Philippines, LT Pete Munro and I sat on the forward flight deck, our legs hanging over the catwalk. We could see and hear the bow wave as the ship cut swiftly through the sea. There was something very calming about hearing the bow cut softly through the water. The catwalk was a place where many would go to escape the stress of the day. The breeze created by the ship moving forward carried the smell of the smoke and fire aft away from us. We really didn't talk as there was nothing we could say. The loss of our friends was too much. We had some old "C" rations that had been warmed by the fire. They really tasted terrible, but it was the first food, as we had nothing to eat that day.

The flight deck was covered with shipmates; no one wanted to go below to sleep, so we just laid back and went to sleep under the stars knowing how fortunate we were to do so.

My other vivid memory was after the fire. I was down in the forward JO bunk room. It was dark, everything was burned and melted, and had that wet smell of fire. My job was to survey the

gear of two of our pilots we lost in the fire, LTJG Tom Spitzer and ENS Ron "Chico" Tardio.

I separated personal gear from Navy gear and packed the personal gear in a newly made plywood box, specially made for this job. As I went through Chico's gear, I felt guilty as if I was a voyeur. I was invading his personal space, his privacy. I had to look through everything and make sure that anything being sent back to his family wouldn't reflect poorly on

the memory of him or cause needless pain for his family. Little did I know that this was practice for doing this same job many times on my '67 cruise.

Scotty and Fritz saved my life that day as did an unknown shipmate who pulled me out of the deep water in the hangar bay. I had tripped and gotten stuck underwater. He helped to save me from drowning, and I never knew who he was.

After leaving the Philippines, we had a funeral at sea. Although this is centuries-old sailing tradition, I had never participated in one. It was very moving seeing the respect of the shipmates as the body slipped into the sea.

I changed my Navy directive to have a burial at sea if there were any parts that needed burying.

CHAPTER SIXTEEN

Heading Home

Most of the squadron pilots flew to Lemoore but, as a new guy, I had to ride the ship back to the states.

There was plenty of administrative work to be done so those of us still on the ship were kept quite busy. We had our evenings off as we had no flight operations and were working 9 to 5 shifts.

The bunk room was only to be used for sleeping, and there was not really a place for us to go since the fire had destroyed the forward areas of the ship. We couldn't use the wardroom except for meals. We had no place to read, play acey-deucy or cards or relax in a chair.

Pete Munro and I were back in the 0-2 bunkroom. We'd lay on the floor listening to music from all our new electronic equipment courtesy of our last visit to Japan. Since the roof still leaked, we had water on the deck. As the ship rolled the water would rush to the low side and then as the ship rolled to the other side, back it would come rushing over our legs as we listened to the music.

We eventually docked at Coronado Naval Air Station, San Diego to off-load the aircraft. While the airplanes were being off-loaded and made ready to fly, we had a couple of days to relax in San Diego where the Navy had a large presence.

What amazed me, and something I didn't expect, was that there was no acknowledgement of us as returning, combat veterans.

No "Hello, how are you? What was it like? Or, "How are you coping?" No one said, "Would you like a cup of coffee?"

Nothing.

Everybody was doing their own thing, partying, watching tv, and so forth. I got truly angry and got into a couple of fights. I was not a happy camper.

When I returned from my yet-to-come cruises, I noticed the same reaction from those returning for the first time. Since this was still early in the war, they weren't calling me names, spitting on me or keying my car—which happened to me later. So, I guess this wasn't too bad for my first return.

We had about eight airplanes fit for duty. I was one of the pilots selected to fly an aircraft to Lemoore Naval Air Station, our new home for the next several months.

I was "Tail-End Charlie" in the formation of the four airplanes in the division. About halfway to Lemoore I had severe vibrations, my speed dropped, and I couldn't maintain altitude. I radioed my lead, "Fritz" and said I had a problem. While he was returning to join on me, I could see that the external fuel tank on my right wing was no longer attached in the front and was now angled sideways to the direction of flight. This was causing extremely high drag. Fritz joined and viewed the problem and we both agreed that I had to try and release the tank; we checked to make sure nothing below us would be damaged by a tank falling from the sky. I was lucky that the electrical connections to the release weren't damaged and off it came. We marked were it landed so the squadron could come back and recover the tank. We both landed safely. Finally, home.

CHAPTER SEVENTEEN

Squadron Refit: 1967

With the loss of four of our pilots in the fire, and many others having reached their combat limit, we had a lot of new pilots joining the squadron. A few of us with combat experience remained

to help all our new pilots. I was assigned as a wingman to Lieutenant Commander (LCDR) Don Davis.

A very experienced A-4 pilot, he had the most hours in the A-4 at the time. Don was a great mentor. He wanted me to be the best A-4 pilot in all disciplines and explained how to improve where I needed it.

Another pilot new to our squadron was LCDR Jerry "Felter" Breast. He had been in Navy squadron VX-5 developing bomb delivery methods, mil settings for bombs, as well as other delivery methods for many different ordnances. He helped all of us with our bombing techniques.

LCDR. Jerry "Felter" Breast. Photo by the Author.

He was from Tennessee, and he just couldn't say "Animal"; he made it three syllables "An Dy Mule," which later caused a problem. His wife was Ophelia; throughout the time he was with the squadron, I didn't know her true name. Jerry "Felter" eventually rose to the rank of Admiral. The squadron was filling up with good pilots, excellent people to call your friends. We worked 14-18-hour days preparing for the return to the war.

We did get breaks; the Navy had started to allow some junior officers the freedom to live off base. Dave Carey and I moved into an apartment in Hanford, CA, a town close to the base. It was comfortable living compared to living in the BOQ. We had not only a bedroom but a living room and a kitchen, too! I have always enjoyed cooking, so I cooked many of the meals for both of us, or just me, depending on our schedule. Dave got serious with a lady whom he ended up marrying after his return from being a POW. More on

My N3N.

that later. I wasn't planning on any relationship until I ended my combat career. I met too many young widows. I felt they had been cheated. I didn't want the responsibility of thinking about another person. I concentrated on saving my own butt.

I had been thinking of hobbies. I had already used the base auto shop to tune up my car; there had to be something out there for a hobby. As a kid, dad and I made flying model airplanes, but that didn't hold the same interest. I started perusing "Trade-a-Plane" just to see what was out there and I found a nice N3N, an old Navy biplane trainer.

Just the thing, eh?

It was in Twinkletown, Mississippi. I got permission to fly a training flight to Naval Air Station Memphis and took a bus to Twinkletown and Jack Adams' Aircraft sales. I didn't know that Jack was the first private-aircraft salesman, an old duster pilot and a Delta Air Lines pilot (a company in my future).

The plane was in good shape and cost $3500. The bank wouldn't lend me the money for the airplane, but gave me a car loan instead. Now I only had to get back to Twinkletown and fly her back to Hanford.

I requested a week of leave from the Navy. When I got back to Twinkletown, Jack gave me a quick checkout in the airplane, a full tank of gas and a gallon of oil to take with me. What I didn't know was that the old radial engines, like the one in this airplane, went through oil about as fast as the gas. This was the same type of engine as was in Lindbergh's "Spirit of St. Louis." A reliable engine that just used lots of oil.

Jack presented me with a highway map and marked where there were some duster strips where I could land and get fuel. I didn't have a parachute and couldn't afford to buy one. There was no radio, just a tarp and sleeping bag. Jack said the dusters along the way would update as to the next landing strip.

What a way to see the states. Low and slow for four days; each day was three, three-hour legs limited by oil consumption.

Had I filed a flight plan, it would have looked like this: Arkansas, overnight near Dallas, then Abilene, Odessa and overnight at El Paso. That was followed by a landing in Deming, New Mexico, in a dust storm. I put down behind a hangar, since the wind was too strong to stall the plane for landing—a trick taught to me by my initial flight instructor, a WWI veteran, air mail and barnstorming pilot. I learned a lot from old Lloyd.

I flew across New Mexico and Arizona, then just west of San Diego I banked north to Hanford and made it in time for the Monday's All Officers Meeting (AOM). I didn't get in trouble, this time.

The squadron moved to Fallon, Nevada for several weeks of night and day bombing practice followed by our annual nuclear-weapon qualifications.

The squadron was working its tail off. We were getting little sleep and becoming very tired. Our time to head back to combat was ever closer. The time to fly back onto the Mighty O for carrier quals and general work with the ship was nearing.

Now in addition to storing my car, I had to find someone to care for the plane. Fortunately, there were several duster pilots based at Hanford, and they promised to look after her.

CHAPTER EIGHTEEN

Departing the States

The squadron moved aboard *Oriskany* in early June 1967 while she was docked at the Naval Air Station Alameda in Oakland California.

Across the bay was San Francisco. After we finished our chores, we went over to the big city. The hippies hadn't yet taken over the whole city, so it was much like a western sin city. A fun place for a young Navy pilot—not too expensive, with many attractions to keep one busy.

A tradition that I enjoyed was stopping at Heinold's First and Last Chance Saloon for the final drink before returning to the ship.

Jack London studied in this bar and the owner helped him go to the University of California Berkley. The floor is slanted because of the 1906 earthquake; an enjoyable stopping point. I made sure that it was the last place I visited before sailing to Vietnam.

The author in a 1967 photo. Photographer: "Fritz" Schroeder.

On 16 June we set sail, sliding out under the Golden Gate Bridge, looking up at her from our decks. An unusual view, but one that I always remember: leaving to an uncertain future.

As we steamed toward Hawaii, we spent our days getting ready for everything we could consider. In Hawaii we were to be given an Organizational Readiness Inspection (ORI) to ensure we were ready for combat. Flight operations commenced when we were 300 miles from Hawaii. The first mission was to fly a simulated nuclear-bombing profile into the Islands, hitting the target on *Kahoolawe* on time and in the target circle. I was flying 50 feet above the water at 360 knots. Ahead, this mountain started to rise out of the water. I had found Hawaii, just as a hand on a century-old sailing ship might have seen it.

After I finished my qualification, Don led me on an airborne tour. Lush green islands dotted the sea and nothing else except blue water. What a way to be introduced to this wonderful place.

There was a tremendous amount of Naval history in Hawaii. We anchored at Pearl Harbor. We sailed in local waters for our inspection which we passed—or otherwise they wouldn't let us go to war?

We had 24 hours to enjoy the beaches, and I was able to do a little sailing with LT Dale "Step" Landroth. ("Step-and-a-half" was his full nickname, because Dale was noticeably short. We teased that it took him a step and a half to keep up.)

He was a good friend, even though he did lead me astray at times.

LT. Dale "Step" Landroth. Author's photo.

We rented an outrigger canoe with sail and launched off the beach through the breaking surf. Little did we know that this would be the last of fun-filled days. The ship set sail for the Philippines, our last stop before combat.

As before, we flew the planes off early for maintenance and washing. Setting up in the BOQ we had Fritz test out the newest flight gloves. With all his flight gear on he jumped into the pool to see if he could operate the fittings to release the parachute. The rest of us just watched from poolside with a beer and hotdog.

Bets were taken to see if the gloves worked or if he would drown. Having advanced knowledge that I would not disclose, I bet he would drown. I won some good money, but I lost my beer and dog jumping in to save him. The gloves didn't work, so as before, we flew without hand protection.

LTJG Fritz Schroeder. Photo by the author.

Oriskany was designated flagship of Carrier Division Nine in Subic Bay, 9 July, and we set sail for Yankee Station.

PART IV

Back a Second Time

Die with memories, not dreams.
Unknown

By summer of 1967, the war has changed and intensified. By now the Vietnamese had plenty of experience firing and guiding these SA-2 missiles. And they now come up in salvos of two, sometimes three. VA-163 photo.

117

CHAPTER NINETEEN

Rules of the War: 1967

The rules, under which we trained, had been changed. Washington now controlled, to a very great degree, our targets, routes to the targets, and times to hit those targets.

And the targets were now in the more restricted areas (according to a priority scale developed at the beginning of the bombing). The most critical targets were "A," or under the phonetic code "Alpha."

Strikes against these were then known as "Alpha" strikes, and usually they entailed the entire Air Wing. Many times, they were coordinated with another carrier and the US Air Force.

They would plan as many as three air strikes a day: 0800, 1200 and 1500 hours. Each pilot would fly two of the three missions. There was no real consistency planning the missions. For days we might have Alpha strikes; then back to the recce role and 12-hour day/night shifts.

This put quite a strain on us; we were constantly tired. The only rest we got was when we lost planes to combat; there would be a few extra pilots who didn't have to fly. These were significant changes that didn't take into account the adaptations the Vietnamese made, or would make, knowing we would still be bombing. We would need to change our planning, requiring we change our tactics and approach to these targets. Having this information in advance would have helped to cut our losses.

Whenever we got within about 20 miles from the target, they had missiles flying at three times the speed of sound and level with us.

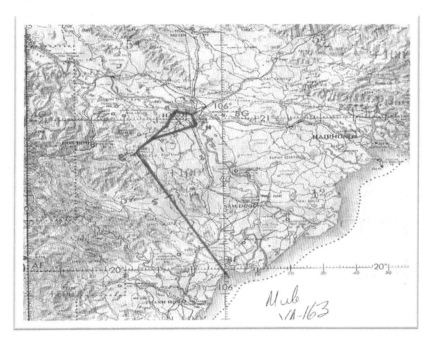

These were Russian SA-2 missiles with a 440-pound warhead. The mobile launchers were usually deployed in a six-point-star arrangement, with a missile on a launcher at each point of the star, and with the radar guidance in the center of the missile site.

Each missile had a booster rocket for launch. The missile was not guided until the booster dropped off, exposing the antenna for radar guidance. They were armed before launch for one of three types of detonation: contact fusing which meant hitting an object;

command detonation, controlled by the radar operator; or VT fusing, a fuse emitting a radar signal to explode at a certain distance set before launch. Our five-inch, Zuni rockets had contact or VT fusing. The missile warhead had a kill radius of 210 feet and damage out to 350 feet. With the forward vector of the missile, this created an ever-expanding cone of deadly flak. If you happened to be in the center of the blast, the damage could be much less.

A SAM site. VA-163 photo.

The next layer of defense was the heavy 57mm and 85mm guns, fused to detonate at our roll-in altitude, filling the sky with flak we had to fly through. Then as we established our dive angle, they had a four-barrel 23mm rapid fire gun (6,000 rounds per minute) peppering us while we were in the dive. It sounded like popcorn popping as we flew through it. The last layer was the 37mm gun, fused to detonate at our pull-off altitude which was usually between 3000-4000 feet altitude. After leaving the target area they usually left us alone.

We hadn't trained for this type of event, and our formation didn't allow us good maneuvering room. We started losing men and planes daily. As we gained experience with these new challenges, we changed our tactics.

We no longer flew as a four-plane formation but flew in two-plane sections, spread farther apart, allowing the freedom of looking at everything around you instead of just looking at keeping in position on a lead plane. This also allowed you to see the blind spot behind your section mate's airplane in case a missile was tracking him from behind. These changes helped immensely, but still overall, the missiles, guns and MiG's took their toll.

The A-4 could carry a payload of 6,000 pounds of bombs: five, 1,000-pounders and two, 500-pounders but no extra fuel; this became a standard load if you were assigned as a bombing aircraft on the Alpha strike. If you were assigned as a Flak Suppressor, the normal preferred load was six Zuni packs, four Zuni's to a pack.

Zuni rockets firing. Author's photo.

That load made for easier maneuvering to get more shots at enemy emplacements firing at the strike group. The Zuni was a point-and-shoot weapon; it eliminated having to climb back to altitude to make a bombing run. Our sister squadron, VA-164, was trained to use a new anti-radar weapon called the "Shrike." VA-164 had several aircraft equipped with the Shrike as well as bombing aircraft.

The USAF usually used the F-105 "Thunder Jet" as its bomber. (Since they made a "Thud" noise when hitting the ground after being hit, we knew them as "Thuds"). They carried many different types of ordnance, and many times were on target with us. They suffered many losses; the "Thud" didn't take a hit as well as the A-4.

CHAPTER TWENTY

Back On the Line: 1967

On the morning of 11 July, we arrived on "Yankee Station." We were getting ready to be in place to take up our combat role on 14 July. On 12 July we started flying some warmup hops to get us

The Angel. Photo by the author.

ready for the big event.

The Saints' first operational loss occurred when LT Don "Woody" Wood got a bad cat shot and had to eject just off the bow.

The "Angel" helicopter rescued Woody; he was wet, unhurt and a bit upset. We were down one plane before we even got started. Not the best way to begin our cruise, but at least we had our pilot back.

It was 14 July and on the first launch of the day we lost an aircraft. Our sister squadron, VA-164, had sent a section of two against a small bridge. LTJG Larry Cunningham, one of my buddies, got hit by a 37mm round. He lost the nose of his aircraft, and with it, his radio and electronics. Without a radio or navigation gear, he made it back to *Oriskany*. His aircraft was on fire, but he didn't know it. He was setting up in the pattern to come aboard, but he lost control when he lowered his flaps. He ejected and was rescued just aft of the ship by that same Angel helicopter.

My first mission was an Alpha Strike. After we launched, we

Our Skipper: CDR Bryan "Magnolia" Compton. Author's photo.

all rendezvoused with Magnolia in the lead of the strike group.

LT Russ Kuhl was the Skipper's wingman; LCDR. Don Davis the section leader and I was on his wing. We flew the standard formation for a four-plane division, a fingertip four (a jet at each fingertip), close to each other and not the most maneuverable formation.

We had just gone "feet dry" when the missiles came straight at us: level, big, fast and a big fireball pushing them. We didn't really have time to react; fortunately, they passed through us and didn't explode. I can still remember the look in Don's eyes when we got back to the ship. His first combat mission, first missile encounter and a very scary one it was. We were lucky that the missiles missed or didn't explode; otherwise, we would have had losses.

Don and I launched again for a recce flight. Compared to the morning mission, it was not nearly as exciting. Just some 37mm flak to contend with that wasn't very accurate. All things considered, you could say it was a relaxing flight.

On 15 July I was scheduled for two hops. The first was another recce, which is usually not a stressful event. Generally, we encountered 37mm flak and the guns did not have radar guidance. If they got lucky you might get hit. When we did get hit, you just had to hope it didn't hit anything vital. I had a small bullpup missile on my right wing and used it to good effect on a railcar. I didn't really care for the bullpup missile. You had to follow directly behind it; it is a line-of-sight weapon, which we guided with a side-stick controller on the left side of the cockpit. You had to follow the missile until it hit the target; you can't maneuver the aircraft, and that makes you an easier target. The hole in my plane was confirmation of that. My second hop was a tanker hop, just topping off anyone who needed fuel making sure they all recovered safely and then checking out the next tanker after his launch. We lost another pilot, LTJG Rob Cassell from VA-152: KIA, to anti-aircraft fire (AAA).

On 16 July I was again scheduled for a 2-hop day. The first was an Alpha to Phu Ly railyard. The SAMs were plentiful, one hitting LCDR Butch Verich of VF-162. He had to eject, successfully evaded the enemy on the ground and was rescued by an HS-2 helicopter from the *USS Hornet*. On the second mission we found some trucks; to keep the Skipper happy, and to show that we weren't wasting taxpayer's money, we left them burning. In summary, day three on the line, with three planes down and one pilot killed was not a great beginning.

On 17 July we were scheduled for two Alpha strike missions: a small strike force to Ninh Binh and then the Than Hoa Bridge. The target at Ninh Binh was just out of missile range, but we still had to deal with 57mm and 37mm flak. Don's plane sustained a small hole from something and mine was unscathed. We got some good hits on the river traffic, and left several targets burning with black smoke, which meant a petroleum-based materiel, and gray smoke from other supplies.

Our second strike was to the famous "Than Hoa Bridge," a combination rail and motor vehicle bridge.

It was a sturdy monster originally built by the French during their colo-

nial period and then destroyed by the Viet Minh in 1957. It became the pride of the North Vietnamese; they spent seven years rebuilding it, and Ho Chi Minh attended at its dedication in 1964.

Author photos of the Than Hoa Bridge before and during attack.

It had previously been bombed by the Air Force as well as other Navy units, but it was still operational. They had some 37mm gun emplacements at both ends of the bridge. Since this was their pride and joy, their best gunners were manning the guns. We got good hits on the bridge, but after-strike photos showed the bridge still standing. (We believed that if we destroyed the bridge the war would be over.)

FUBAR is an acronym developed during WW II, and its full wording is beyond the scope of this story and inappropriate for younger readers. The Alpha strike on the Co Trai bridge on 18 July was an example of how things can be FUBAR.

The Co Trai Bridge was another tough one. After numerous raids,
it was finally destroyed. US Navy photo.

Our four-plane division bombs were fully capable of bringing down the Co Trai Bridge. Inbound to the target we were above a low cloud cover. Our anti-radar guidance equipment would give us an audible sound of the tracking radar. Each radar had its own specific signal which identifies what type of radar; a different radar signals is used for a specific mission: controlling a radar guided gun, a missile tracking radar, and a different radar for missile guidance. Listening to these sounds told us what threat we were facing.

The radar signature changed to guidance, indicating that a missile or missiles were launched. I knew that we would have little time to react when it came through the clouds. Be it due to anxiety or being hyper-alert, my eyelids fluttered.

We were flying in the fingertip formation, and I had to maintain my station, which would not allow me to look at my surroundings. Suddenly, a missile broke through the clouds. As we trained in the States, the Skipper rolled into a steep downward spiral, and the formation followed. The missile roared past, just missing the front of Skipper's right wing, and exploded as it passed us. We began a climb back to an altitude suitable for bombing runs as we returned to our original route to the bridge. The flak defending the target was heavy, and we were so low still that our bombing runs were so short it made aiming hard.

As we rolled in on the target, the popcorn sound was very loud; I knew they had me in their sights.

Upon return to the ship, we learned that LCDR Dick Harman was on the ground evading the enemy. LTJG Larry "Duth" Duthie, a good friend was recovered that afternoon by a USAF Jolly Green helicopter. He had been taken to a secret base in Laos.

Rescue efforts were now underway for Dick. The Jolly Green had diverted Duth to Laos. It was refueled, leaving Duth alone in a shack on the runway while it returned to pick up Dick. The Jolly Green and its A-1 Spad escorts were unsuccessful because a Navy Admiral denied them permission to enter Route Package VIa. Another Jolly Green was sent from Udorn, Thailand to pick up Duth from that little base in Laos.

Dick was now on top of a steep ridge and somewhat separated from the enemy. A rescue attempt with a small Navy HU-2 Clementine helicopter (like the Angel that rescued Don Wood a week earlier) resulted in that helicopter seriously shot up; it barely made it back to the deck of a Navy destroyer.

There was discussion about trying a rescue attempt that involved dropping a canister holding a balloon that he could fill with helium, let it float with a cable attached to him. A C-130 aircraft with a special recovery system would then snag the balloon and the cable thus popping Dick off the ground and up into the air. The idea was that the cable would be retracted to bring him into the airplane. A better plan was needed.

During the night of Dick's shootdown, a scheme was approved for the morning of 19 July. LCDR Leon "Bud" Edney of VA-164 was to lead the recovery mission. There were three coordinated parts to the plan: An SH-3 Big Mother helicopter from The *USS Constellation* would launch in the dark morning to arrive over Dick's location with the rising sun. It was to be escorted by four Lockets, A-1 Spads, from VA-152, and they were responsible for navigating to the valley near Dick's position. When they arrived, Bud Edney would launch a "Willie Pete" smoke rocket indicating Dick's location.

Don and I would be up high with several other A-4s to provide cover for the helicopter. A diversionary strike was also planned nearby to divert the enemy's attention.

The variable we couldn't control was the effort the enemy would mount to defeat the rescue. They knew we would come to save Dick, so they were well prepared, and they had brought in more guns.

Don and I had separated and were flying in a big circle above the valley. I had six Zuni packs on board. Don had bombs. We were instructed not to attack the enemy until after the helicopter had Dick aboard, and only then to keep the guns off the helicopter. If Dick wasn't picked up, we were not to hit the area so they wouldn't be motivated to kill Dick when they found him.

As I saw the helicopter enter the valley, Bud was in his dive launching the smoke rocket. As he did, smoke on another ridge (some thought someone may have fired a Zuni) caused confusion for the helicopter crew. Big Mother had overflown Dick's location and had turned out into the valley.

The area below looked to be completely covered in the white flak of 37mm rounds. While Bud was trying to direct the helicopter crew back toward the ridges surrounding the valley, they were radioing that they were taking hits. It really hurts to remember their voices, which were followed by the helicopter exploding in a big fireball and dropping down out of the sky. I was sick to my stomach. It was very a traumatic experience, and one I still see in my mind these 50-some years later.

By this time, I had lost visual contact with Don, he said he was heading back to the ship. I told him I would follow shortly. It was taking me a while to gather myself; I had these Zunis and I knew where I wanted to go. The Than Hoa bridge wasn't too far away and I remembered exactly where those 37mm gun emplacements were.

This was the perfect weapon to attack them, so that is what I did. They weren't expecting anyone; the guns were silent for my first two runs, I wanted to wait until they began to fire; I wanted to shoot at someone, not just a gun. They targeted me, and I got some particularly good hits with the Zunis. I started climbing to leave, and noticed an object sailing at me. It looked like a missile but there was no fireball behind it. I tried to maneuver so it would miss me. I thought I had been successful until the rear of my airplane lifted. There was no indication that I had a problem so I just headed for the water as quickly as I could.

The whole airwing was short on fuel. VA-164 pilot LTJG Barry Wood had flak damage, was leaking fuel, ran out of fuel and he ejected. A USAF KC-135 tanker heard our guys calling on guard frequency about the fuel problem. The tanker had a drogue re-fueling system in addition to the standard USAF system. The drogue is the system used by Navy aircraft. He diverted to give us a hand. He was a life saver. We heard the USAF tried to court-martial him for diverting, but the Navy wanted to give him a medal. The Air Force wisely backed off. He did what was right and saved American pilots.

CDR. Herb Hunter, the executive officer for VF-162, one of our F-8 squadrons, had been hit. He couldn't get rid of a stuck bomb and couldn't raise his wing, which was needed to allow the plane to slow to a safe landing speed. He was low on fuel and had run out of options, so he tried to land on the *USS Bon Homme Richard.* They rigged the barricade to stop him on the deck, but he was so fast he cut through it like melted butter and was killed. I added to the problems of the day; I was running out of fuel. The strike force had recovered, allowing the O-Boat to launch an A-4 buddy-tanker. My good friend and squadron mate, LTJG Gordon "Goose" Hunter was the pilot. I was at a higher altitude to save as much fuel as I could

and saw Goose on the cat. I got him to switch to squadron frequency after he launched. I instructed him to climb in a tight circle around the ship and deploy the drogue; I would descend and refuel. I could keep the power at idle so as not to burn much fuel. I dropped my ram air turbine (RAT) to keep electrical power in case I flamed out. My engine started running roughly; I hooked up and began the refueling process. It was so nice to see the fuel gauge slip upward. When I got 1000 pounds of fuel, we separated at a low altitude. When I recovered, I gave the maintenance chief a thumbs up signal that the airplane was good to go; he returned a thumbs down, and I wondered why. It seemed I had a large rip in the center-line fuel tank, almost splitting it in half.

I was taken to the Admiral's quarters and had to explain to my Skipper, CAG, the ship's Captain and the Admiral how in the "H" that happened. I had better fess up to what I had done. I explained that we were under orders not to attack the enemy until the helicopter had Dick aboard and was heading home. We were to protect it from ground fire. That didn't happen and since I was intently watching the helicopter enter the area and watched the event unfold, I lost track of my lead. I found myself alone with all this armament and I knew where I could use it productively. I went to Than Hoa. I waited until they finally started shooting so I had a good target. That was when the missile and I had our encounter. Since my aircraft had been moved by the object and there were paint marks on the tank, we determined that I and the missile had hit each other. A mid-air encounter. That seemed to satisfy everyone, and I didn't get in trouble.

What a day. A helicopter with four souls aboard lost, an ex-Blue Angel dead, two more aircraft lost and the state of a downed pilot unknown. Dick was later declared dead on return of the POWs.

We abandoned the fingertip-four formation, breaking into two-plane sections to give us more freedom of movement, and applied this new strategy to the morning Alpha strike on 20 July. During the launch, LTJG Jim "Oar" Nunn VF-162 went off the bow into the water. What a start to the day. Our target was the My Xa petroleum storage facility 15 miles northwest of Haiphong. The flak was heavy and the Skipper's wingman LT Russ Kuhl, got hit but made it to water. He was rescued but had an injury to his neck which required that he be moved to the hospital at Cubi Point, which is where LTJG Larry "Duth" Duthie had been taken with an injured leg.

My second mission was an eight-plane strike to a supply depot south of Than Hoa.

Don was our leader, and I on his wing. Don's radio failed and he signaled to me to take the lead. We approached the well-defined target and took a picture of it. They weren't shooting at us, so I changed our roll-in point and planned on a 30-degree dive, which gives better accuracy than a 45-degree dive.

Author's photos. Left, the supply depot "before," and below, the supply depot "after our visit."

We coasted down and all four of us had great hits on the target. I took a picture of it as we left: some black smoke from petroleum products, and gray smoke from supplies that was visible from 35 miles away. We were pleased with the result; Don gave me a big hug. His hard work in making me a better pilot was paying off. I felt like I was becoming a professional at this war business.

If nobody is shooting at you, it's a good day; 21 July was a very good day. I had two hops as a tanker. I launched as one of the first aircraft and joined up with the other tanker. He hooked up to my drogue and took some fuel to ensure I could refuel someone; both of us covered the landings; he was the last to recover. I was available to returning aircraft, giving them fuel as needed. I repeated the checkout of the newly launched tanker and then landed.

I flew two hops on 22 July: a recce hop, in RPII and night tanker duty. During the recce hop, 37mm guns were taking their shots at me. When there was only one firing, it was not too difficult to stay clear of them; but if they did hit you, they do a lot of damage. You just had to be smart about ducking them and keep the plane moving to make it hard to track or anticipate your next position.

The second hop, as the night duty tanker was as always, a challenge. Night landings and night tanker duty on a moonless night were more stressful than getting shot at. They wired some pilots up to watch heart rates and confirmed this.

Two more hops on 23 July. We flew into RP III, a big area that included Vinh. I'm not sure why, but Vinh was a real hot spot. The gunners there were numerous and accurate. Our strategy was to isolate it by cutting the roads leading in and out, which was the best way to stay alive. I think most of the guns in that southern section of RP III were in Vinh; beyond the immediate area, the threat around it was less, and we could concentrate on getting good hits.

My second flight was another night tanker. As the duty pumper you had to fly a narrow window of airspeed and keep the aircraft as level as possible. Too fast and the drogue would ride up putting the tanking pilot in your engine exhaust path, which was very rough air; if you were too slow, it made for a bad angle to get the refueling aircraft probe into the basket. I enjoyed the challenge and worked hard to give my buddies the best shot at getting the fuel they needed.

We went back to RP III on 24 July for a single mission. The enemy had learned to avoid daytime movement of equipment, fuel or anything else. We didn't see any movement, so we went after small bridges, which had sustained previous damage and were in the process of being repaired or replaced with new construction.

I was scheduled for a single mission on 25 July: an early recce with Don. Don had a second hop that night.

One of the many bridges we'd bomb over and over. Author's photo

During that mission, either as a result of being shot by gunners or target fixation, Don's plane flew into the ground, our first KIA. Don's body was returned in 1988, but there was no evidence of what happened.

It was a devastating loss to me. He was my mentor, my leader and a good friend. It really hit me hard as I cried myself to sleep. It was not only me; the whole squadron couldn't believe we lost such an excellent, experienced pilot. The next day I went to the Skipper; he had lost his wingman and his section leader. We were the only ones left in the division; I told him that if we were going to survive, we needed to fly together. I went back on his wing just as in '66. I knew both of us would make it. Later, he appointed me as a section leader, breaking up our team.

I had a double recce on 26 July: daytime and nighttime missions with the Skipper. My bombing had improved, so the Skipper wasn't complaining about me wasting taxpayer money. I was also progressing in my landing skills. I got the target landing wire, the three wire (there are only four wires) and two OK passes. I was near the top of the landing board; I could win some money.

As of 27 July, I had been flying too much, and I was taken off the schedule. It was time to have a popcorn party in my room. I was going to live through the next day. I had an old aluminum, electric

137

popcorn popper from my college days. I bought a 50-pound bag of popcorn from the ship store and a 5-gallon tin of oil. When we had a movie night, I made popcorn for the ready room. By the time I finished my third combat tour the popper had worn out.

I was scheduled for an Alpha strike on 28 July. Our target was the Hai Duong solders' barracks, situated between Haiphong and Hanoi. An obvious hot spot with the regular mix of missiles and heavy flak. I was on the wing of the Commander of the Air Wing (CAG); he led the strike. We got good hits on the target, doing our job as was expected. That evening we lost an A-3 from VAH-4, with two KIA and one rescued, so our bad luck continued. I had another popcorn party because I was scheduled to be the squadron duty officer (SDO) on 29 July.

An Alpha strike was planned for 30 July. It was a joint mission involving four of our A-4s led by Magnolia and four USAF Thuds. The target was Bac Gang, 20 nautical miles northeast of Hanoi. The main rail line from China went through Bac Giang to Hanoi. The strike had four USAF "Thuds" attacking just before we came in with our four A-4s. I was on Magnolia's wing. The Thuds rolled in on their attack; three of the planes went down and the fourth was on fire, heading for the water. Our formation had made it through at least 30 missiles. The flak was very heavy, and the popcorn sound was deafening loud during my dive-bombing run. LCDR Jerry Breast was hit by a 57mm putting a few holes in his plane. As we left, I tried to get a picture of the rail damage, but the firing was too hot to do anything but keep the airplane jinking (moving erratically).

"There's no rest for the . . .," well, you know the rest of it. On 31 July we went directly into the fire and didn't waste time in the frying pan: An Alpha to Hanoi, the most heavily defended city in the world.

One couldn't count the missiles launched, there were too many, you just had to keep ducking them. During our approach and attack, LTJG Charlie Zuhoski, VF-111, went down.

An F-8 on fire with a Sidewinder missile burning off. VA-163 photo.

One of the F-8 pilots tried to warn me about a missile tracking me, but he couldn't get out my call sign of "An...dy...mule" out in time.

It blew up in front of my right wing. In in my mind some 50 years later, I still see the missile exploding, the casing coming off and streaking at me. I was enveloped in heavy smoke, the aircraft warning lights lit up, and yet I was still flying. I was stunned for a second, but I heard the Skipper telling me to get back to maneuvering my plane. We finally made it to our roll-in point, dove toward the ground, and released our payloads. All my bombs released, for which I was forever thankful. After we returned to the ship and heard the F-8 pilot's story, my call sign was shortened to "Mule."

August started off with a big bang. During an Alpha strike on Haiphong, I was tracked by a missile, which exploded off my left front. I took a picture of the resulting explosion. The other occurrence that made 1 August special was receiving my first letter since leaving the states.

The second of August was a popcorn-party day. We were scheduled for two hops on 3 August. In the morning we ran a strike on Loi Dong; in the Haiphong area. I got good hits, but some 37mm flak put hole in my left wing and punctured my fuel tank. The A-4 has a sealed fuel bag behind the cockpit area, so I had more than enough fuel to return safely to the ship.

The afternoon hop was a recce to the islands situated along the coast between Haiphong and the port of Cam Pha. I scored some good bomb hits, sinking a couple of boats with other craft sustaining damage.

Above are some barges nestled in among the edges of one of the thousands of islands up north. To the right is an exploding SAM warhead like the one that hit Ralph.

The next day was a mixed bag. I had a good recce hop in the morning, taking out a bridge and another barge.

In the afternoon we returned to the Haiphong area for another petroleum (POL) storage area at Luc Nong.

My roommate, LTJG Ralph Bisz, was hit by a missile. His plane exploded in flight. We didn't see a chute or pick up an emergency beeper. The squadron listed him as KIA, but the Navy classified him as a POW. When the POWs were returned without Ralph, he was declared dead. His body was returned in 2008 and he was interred at Arlington with full honors. His family was gone, but ten of his Saints family attended.

We put our POW bracelets in the casket with him so he would know he was remembered.

LTJG Ralph Bisz. Photo by the author.

It by now became apparent that our missions were changing; targets were being assigned and carefully managed by people in Washington, D.C.

They intended to step up the pressure on the North Vietnamese. We were getting scheduled for two and three Alpha strikes a day, and none of these targets had been attacked previously. They were in the area stretching from Hanoi to Haiphong, the most heavily defended ground ever.

We were fighting MiGs, missiles, big guns that could reach us at altitude and rapid-firing guns during our bombing runs. The 37s were layering our pullout altitude with their dangerous white flak puffs.

On these strikes we were loaded mostly with five 1,000-pound bombs and two 500-pound bombs. Our weight on the cat was over 12 tons, yet our engine just had a little over eight thousand pounds of thrust. We didn't have the power available to go in at low altitudes and then climb to a roll-in altitude and get to 450 knots speed by 5,000 feet above the target, our drop altitude. A 1,000-pound bomb will throw shrapnel over 2,000 feet into the air; we risked getting hit by our own bombs if we weren't out of the dive and above the target by at least 3,000 feet. Washington was trying to control our routes into the target, which put us in harm's way with longer flight times. The less time we were exposed, the less time they had to shoot at us. We went in as directly as we could. Each pilot was usually on the schedule for two of the three Alphas. Target times were again assigned by Washington: 1000, 1400, and 1600 hours; consistent and so predictable.

Weekends made no difference for combat assignments. On Saturday, 5 August, I was scheduled for one Alpha. Our target was a SAM site at Quang Yen. The gunners defending were damn good shooters which affected our hits on the target. We got fair hits, but the site's defenses prevented a surgical strike. We did not destroy the site completely. My plane sustained another hole but nothing incapacitating.

The next day was all night flying: two-night hops, with the Skipper going to places I couldn't talk about then and still won't.

They didn't usually shoot missiles at us at night, but that didn't stop the gunners. On debrief I gave them the standard story which makes everyone feel better: we went to the assigned area, we bombed some trucks, used a 45-degree bombing angle and released at 5,000 feet. Sometimes we added that we had them burning.

Because we were up all night on 6 August, we could sleep in on 7 August. We left the line on 8 August for a short trip to the Philippines and Cubi Point. It was only a month since we sailed from there, 9 July. It seemed like a lifetime ago.

CHAPTER TWENTY-ONE

R&R: Cubi Point

At 1600 the next day, 9 August, we moored to a harbor buoy; we took liberty boats ashore. Lieutenant Moose Lundy was finished with his combat time, and we had plans for a grand party at the Subic Bay Officers' club.

This was the elite club, and we made a mess of it that evening. We called ourselves the Champagne squadron; each of us bought a bottle of champagne. Before we popped the cork, we shook them, aimed at each other, called "missiles away" and sent corks flying. Then we drank what was left. A good send-off for a nice guy and terrific pilot.

After a week on shore leave, hung over from another night of drinking, we left for Yankee Station. I got in a maintenance test hop; the aircraft checked out in good shape. I was now the line division officer, a member of the brown shirts. The flight deck is choreographed as precisely as the New York Ballet.

Brown shirts are responsible for the plane while it is not flying. They ride the brakes if it is to be moved, they carry the tiedown chains in a bag on their back. The chains are very heavy, and they need to be robust to prevent big airplanes from moving on a pitching deck.

Blue shirts physically move the planes on the flight deck and hangar deck.

Red shirts are responsible for mounting the ordnance and ensuring it will work.

Green shirts perform the maintenance on the plane.

And the yellow shirts direct the movement of the plane when manned, they communicate with the pilot with hand signals during the day and flashlight-wands at night.

There is no radio communication during all this, just hand signals.

After landing, the planes are parked forward. After the recovery is complete, the crews manually move all the planes aft to the landing area where they are fueled, the ordnance is loaded, and maintenance, if needed, is done.

Then when we man them, the yellow shirts direct our planes to the cats for launch.

The safety record on aircraft carriers is second to none. The sailors do this eight times a day, launching some ten to twenty planes each launch.

The interdependence of all these roles results in a finely tuned, proficient process.

The jets I flew were maintained by 18 to 20-year-old sailors. They worried the whole time I was out on a mission, praying for my safe return. When a pilot didn't return, they wondered and worried that they might have been responsible.

The flight deck was not only dangerous for them physically, but played on their minds as well. These young sailors had very demanding and responsible jobs. They deserved the respect of the pilot group, and we gave it to them.

CHAPTER TWENTY-TWO

On the Line: Our Second Go

I was back on the line 18 August and flew with new ordnance called "Walleye," a TV-guided bomb that, while still attached to the aircraft, sent a visual image of the target to our yellow and black radar scope in the cockpit to aim it. The display was horrible.

Our squadron purchased small, battery-powered Sony TVs and modified them to fit where the radar scope had been in the instrument panel.

Now we had a useful view. To facilitate locking on a target, we would trail our wingman and align the bombsight on him to see if it locked on the plane. If it didn't, we used the mil-rings to reposition the aim until the bomb locked onto it. Once we got to the real target, we'd put the bombsight on the target, pull the trigger for a lock-on and check to see if it was aiming at the target. The bomb was, essentially, a glider with no onboard course correction.

We still had to get close to the target and we needed a high rate of speed. If the gliding bomb lost much velocity, it would veer off course and hit something else. It was accurate but had no stand-off or remote-control capability. (stand-off or remote-control would allow the piloted airplane more maneuvering capability, something we didn't have in Vietnam then. Exposure would have been less, putting us in less danger)

The next day was one hop with the Skipper, again going some-where "we didn't go." He and I accomplished good results we didn't have, on good targets we didn't see.

The second hop, I was the spare—a manned reserve-pilot; there were no aircraft problems and no need for me to launch. The spare pilot would brief with both sections, would function in the role of leader or wingman depending on which aircraft was bro-ken. That way we would accomplish the mission. It's nice to have an easy day.

Moose and I had shared a three-man room; now that he had left, there were two empty bunks. Dave Carey and Goose Hunter moved in. They were on the bunk-bed side, I was in the bunk welded to the curved side of the ship, giving me some extra room for my party supplies. While we had been in Cubi, I purchased a small refrigerator, so we now had food and ice in the room. Uptown living.

The 20th saw the Skipper and me on a recce; as were heading to the water, he took a hit from a 37mm which took off about three feet of his right aileron. That damage precluded carrier landing, so we diverted to Chu Lai airbase in South Vietnam. The Skipper was leading a big mission to Hanoi the next day and I was to be the ready-spare. The Skipper was more important to the mission and the squadron, so he took my aircraft, leaving me marooned with a bunch of marines. They had A-4s and helicopters and a steel mat-ted runway. Just across a hill, was a big concrete runway, with lots of air-conditioned trailers; that was the USAF side of the base. I slept on the ground in a sandbag hooch. It belonged to a marine buddy, with whom I went through flight training. They had a steak dinner that night, paid for in script; I didn't have script and I couldn't pay with US dollars. My buddy paid for my meal, got me a helmet and a rifle which I had never seen or shot before. If I had to use it, I'd probably be as dangerous to "us" as "them." One thing he did forget to do was brief me on where the bunker was, in case of a rocket attack. He had a night flight so he wouldn't be around much. I went to ground or at least laid down to sleep. Suddenly a siren starts wailing followed by explosions. I stuck my head out of the hooch, didn't see much, didn't really know what I should do, so I laid back down.

Next morning, they were still working on the plane, I went on a helicopter mission with a chopper pilot I had met at dinner. A totally different war was taking place on the ground. The nice thing about being in a single seat aircraft, flying at 450 knots, several thousand feet in the air, was that you didn't see the blood and guts of someone getting hit and the plane blown up; the pilot just doesn't return. Clean, as opposed to what I was seeing here. I was happy to get back on the ground; I didn't really like what happened, but I survived. My plane was ready, and I headed back to sea and a more civilized life.

Two of our aircraft were damaged on the Skipper's mission and couldn't be repaired on board. We were down to six mission-ready airplanes out of the 14 at the outset of our tour. Three aircraft were being repaired onboard. We had lost two pilots KIA, and two to injuries. The next day I was the SDO; the most important job of the day was finding a good movie for the ready room and bringing up my popcorn supplies. A genuinely nice day.

There's an unwritten rule about having two good days in a row: it's not allowed. On 23 August the Skipper and I went on the morning Alpha to Haiphong for a flak suppression mission. We saw only four or five SAMs, but plenty of flak. The older cities in the North were built by the French, and you can still see good examples of the nice architecture. The next day we had bad weather. Visibility was so limited that we didn't see enough ground to determine where we were and had to abandon the mission. Even though the visibility was terrible, that didn't prevent them throwing the 85 and 57 flak up through the clouds. The weather was worse for the next two days, so there were no launches. Two days of not getting shot at was a bit like being in heaven: nice and safe, how can you argue with that?

Weather was still an impediment on 28 August. The strike leader couldn't find the target in Haiphong; I was the section lead and gave him directions, but half of the strike group didn't get on target. I had been to Haiphong several times and was perhaps a bit more familiar with the area; my section dropped on the rail line with good hits. On my second hop I led the section into RP V and most our ordnance dropped on the target without getting hit ourselves.

On the morning of the 29th, I went with the Skipper as his section leader to a SAM site at Bai Lam, north of the Phuc Yen MiG base, which had launched many missiles when we were in the Hanoi area. There were four or more missiles launched at us as we were inbound, one tracked me from behind. I must have been in the exact center of the blast as I was not hit by anything other than part of the missile casing. Lucky again.

We had another Alpha on the morning of 30 August. The target was a rail bridge near Haiphong. We got some good hits, but as we left, sections of the bridge were still standing

LTJG Dave Carey, left, and LCDR Al Stafford,
both shot down by the same missile. Author photo.

I was the SDO on the 31st, and a sad day it was. My roommate Dave and his lead, LCDR Al Stafford, were hit by a missile; both were taken prisoner.

LCDR Dick Perry of our sister squadron, VA-164, was also hit by a SAM, and he turned and made it to the water. But after he ejected, he hung lifeless in his chute. When he was checked by the helicopter crewman lowered to help him, they found him dead.

The helicopter was taking hits, so they couldn't take the time to recover Dick Perry's body.

A second roommate was now gone, a POW. Al was also a POW. Dick a fine, experienced pilot was lost to us all.

Years later at a breakfast with Al and our Flight Surgeon "Doc" Adeeb, during a squadron reunion, I mentioned how I wouldn't fly with a handgun. Al told of how his gun saved him. He landed in a pig sty that was full of shit. He was hurting and assessing his condition, when a bullet hit near his head as he lay in the muck.

He looked up and saw a young boy, the kid who had shot at him. He was trying to reload an old, rusted Japanese rifle. Al pulled out his pistol and pointed it the child, trying to signal him that he would shoot if the kid tried to shoot at him again.

An older woman came up to them, yelling at both the kid and Al. She got the kid to put down the weapon. Al did the same. He was taken prisoner by locals, and someone tried to cut off his finger to get his wedding ring. The woman stopped them. He figured the gun saved his life.

I was now assigned as a section leader, and on 1 September I led my section on a mission into RP V. We nailed a barge on the river and hit a couple of trucks, leaving them burning.

I was SDO on 2 September. The next day we were slated for an Alpha strike back to the Than Hoa bridge. We hit it with all our bombs, but the bridge was strong and resisted our best efforts to destroy it. I had two hops on 4 September (Labor Day); both were Alpha strikes to Haiphong. The first was a rail storage area on the river, and the second was a bridge that was previously not hit.

The author was leading a section of A-4s against the barge in the photo on the left and a truck burning in the photo below. Both photos by the author.

Both targets in the photos below sustained damage from our strikes. The enemy's defenses were the same: missiles on the inbound leg, flak as we dropped on the target and missiles outbound and back to water. Somehow, they seemed to know where we would target next. After I had gotten out of the Navy, I saw pictures in "Life" magazine showing the locals climbing into shelters before we arrived. North Vietnamese did seem to know where we were headed and were well prepared.

The weather deteriorated for the next two days. I flew one weather recce to check our many ground points. We measure the cloud cover, the ceiling of the clouds and the approximate visibility. Our area of responsibility included all areas of North Vietnam, except RP Vl-a.

On the 7th we shifted our attention to RP lll and found some activity on Rt 15. We set four trucks on fire. The next day we returned to what we were now calling "Happy Valley" on RT 15; got another four trucks. It may not sound exciting, but it beats getting nothing but a hole in your airplane. During this period five aircraft were hit by flak. keeping our maintenance crews busy.

Weather interfered with the first mission on the 9th. The next hop was an Alpha to the Red River, which attracted the attention of several SAMs. We ducked in and out of the weather and laid some good hits on the target. Two A-4s were hit, one from each squadron. I don't think there was an unscathed aircraft between our two squadrons. Both squadrons were short of airplanes fit for duty. To get more ordnance on the targets, some planes that were flown only had functional bombing systems. I had to fly without a working radio. I was on the Skipper's wing for that mission; all I had to do was hang on, and I had flown enough with him to do that.

I was in my jet and prepping for a mission on the morning of the 10th and felt like I was getting sick. By the time I closed the canopy, there was no doubt. I cancelled my participation, telling pri-fly that I was sick. At the same I made the call, my buddy Step ejected off the bow due to engine loss. Pri-fly wanted me to repeat what I had said. and the Skipper came on the radio and said, "You heard him." That ended any further discussion as to what I said. I reported to sick bay. I had a fever and was ordered to bed, where I stayed for the next two days. During that time, we had three more damaged planes. CAG was calling our Skipper a senior detachment officer instead of a squadron commander.

I was scheduled for a dark launch on 13 September. The goal was to get to the beach as the sun was rising to assess the weather and its suitability for a mission. The weather was finally improving.

I went on the early morning Alpha and we destroyed a bridge span from one side of the river to the other.

The next days were a combination of weather-cancelled missions and SDO duty. We went off the line on 17 September and steamed to Japan at 1300 hours for some well-deserved R&R. On the way, with Dave's POW status, I sorted through his personal effects for items to be returned to his parents or his fiancée. I composed letters to be included in each parcel that reflected on Dave and his service. Not a fun job. Dave's fiancée, Karen, was really upset and complained that I had read their private correspondence and made some other comments that expressed her pique with me. I didn't respond as I knew she was hurting from Dave's loss. Some years later, I attended their wedding; as we passed through the reception line, Dave asked if I remembered the letter. I told him I did, and he remarked to Karen that he expected that I would.

Dave and Karen Carey on their wedding after Dave's return from POW camp. She waited for him five and a half years. Author's photo.

CHAPTER TWENTY-THREE

To Japan for R&R

We arrived in Japan on 18 September, our first time this year. Some years before, Denny Earl had spent time in Japan as a Mormon missionary. Denny, Goose and I took a week's leave; we visited the towns and people with whom Denny had lived during his mission.

What a way to experience Japan. Our first stop was the train to Osaka where Denny introduced us to the local cuisine. He spoke Japanese, as well as being able to write in Kanji, the Japanese script. Denny was a man of many talents. The next morning, we caught the new, highspeed, Tokaido line, the 120-mph bullet train to Tokyo. To give Goose and me some culture, something we were a bit short of, we went to a Kabuki theater.

The night life in Tokyo was very cool. The next day we went to a Sumo wrestling match and then spent a ton of money in the city. Tokyo was awfully expensive.

We took a slow train to Kanazawa: hard, wooden, straight-backed seats. We stopped at every station—just local color and dried squid to chew on. We arrived late and went to bed. It had been a long but interesting day. At one point, we heard a young Japanese couple talking. Denny said they had just been married and were trying to understand each other. Marriage at that time was arranged by the parents, and they hadn't met until the wedding.

The next day we met with several families. Their daughters escorted and toured with us the rest of the day. We had a nice dinner and then sang songs with them to wrap up the day. Then we met Denny's Kendo (a form of sword fighting with a bamboo stick) teacher.

This is Denny on the right with his Kendo instructor.
The photo of the two appeared in the local newspaper.

The local press published their photo together in the local paper. I guess we never knew Denny was such a celebrity. Again, he was a man of many talents.

The next morning, we took a faster train to Kyoto. I got a good picture of the Golden Pagoda, situated on a small pretty lake, a quiet, beautiful, and calming place.

We flew to Fukuoka and did some clubbing, and I slept the night away on a futon. When we awoke, we took a train back to the ship. The movie that night was "You Only Live Twice."

In a park on the base, I hosted a party for my line division troops.

The Golden Pagoda in Kyoto. Author's photo.

I wanted to show them my appreciation for their hard work. I had extra help in case some of the sailors got too drunk. I didn't want them to get in trouble. It all worked well.

I had finally found the secret to getting drunk three times in a day and yet be sober before going to bed. The Japanese have this system called a hotsy bath. You go to the solon, they put you in a self-contained steam bath with your head sticking out of a hole in the top and a towel around your neck to keep the steam in. Next, they wash you down and stick you in a hole in the ground full of extremely hot water. When you get out, they dry you and you lie down on a table where you receive the best massage you have ever had in your life. You are now sober and off to the bar, again. When you need another drink, you wave this little flag they give you and the waitress runs over with a full drink. When you're drunk you head back to the hotsy bath, and out you come, sober again. Back to the bar, back to the hotsy then to bed. It was a hell of a night. Prior to my return to the line, I was scheduled to go to Atsugi to get an A-4 that had been repaired at the Paint and Repair (PAR) depot.

CHAPTER TWENTY-FOUR

Third Line Period

The ship left on 1 October for our return to Yankee Station. Since I was a maintenance test-pilot, I had to check all the aircraft systems, make sure they functioned correctly before flying a plane to the ship.

My plan was to fly the plane through Naha, Okinawa, the Philippines, and then on to Yankee Station in the Gulf of Tonkin. But when I reported to Atsugi, the plane wasn't ready.

My experience with Denny gave me confidence to travel on the trains, even though I couldn't read the signs. I went to Yokosuka for the day, and on the 2nd to Yokohama. I returned to Atsugi, on 3 October to begin the test flight. My experience from my carrier practice in Lemoore saved me some problems: when I checked the elevator, it didn't move correctly so they shut it down. A cable had not been connected. The test hop is designed to test all the aircraft systems including disconnecting the hydraulic flight controls, climbing to 40,000 feet to check the pressurization, as well as the positive-pressure breathing system in the A-4. You had to learn how to breathe and talk against this pressure. If you had a problem at an extremely high altitude, the pressure increases to get oxygen in your lungs.

The jet stream gets extremely low over Japan, I climbed to 24,000 feet, turned into the wind, dropped my gear and flaps and flew backward across Japan. That was a kick. The plane checked out fine. I went to the club and celebrated. The morning of the 4th I left Atsugi for Naha, Okinawa. Atsugi was a Japanese navy air base in WW ll. The pilots who attacked Pearl Harbor trained there. After the war the base became a US Navy air base. It was interesting to be flying there and Okinawa where famous battles in WW ll were fought. I felt very privileged to be visiting these sites.

It was a two-hour, 48-minute flight to Naha over a lot of water. I used the oldest form of navigating: dead reckoning (DR). I knew where I was when I left the coast of Japan, knew about how fast I was flying over the ground, but had no idea if the wind would cause me to drift right or left of my course. Just had to hope I was correct in my planned course. The A-4 only had a TACAN, a military form of radio navigation. The radio was UHF (Ultra High Frequency) and only used to contact military radios. I had no civilian navigation aids and no ability to talk with other aircraft or a radar controller. I was on my own. I climbed enroute to save fuel. The jet stream is like water flowing in a pipe. The water flowing along the side of the pipe is slower than the water flowing in the center of the pipe. This difference causes a disturbing flow, in aviation terms, turbulence. I climbed until I got turbulence, then descended a few thousand feet. When I was in smooth air, that was as high as was possible and not be affected by the jet stream. I found Okinawa and had radio navigation to the air base. I had a conversation with the first human in a while and was cleared to land. I spent the night on the base.

On 5 October, I left for Cubi Point, Philippines. Some 600 nautical miles of water and my last known navigable point was where I started, Naha. It was a long DR flight plan, about 2 and one-half hours of flying over blue water. From the time I saw the Philippine coast, it took another thirty minutes to get to Cubi and land my aircraft. Another 800+ miles in a hard seat in a small cockpit. The A-4 was not designed for a comfortable three-hour flight.

The A-4's tight cockpit isn't designed for comfort.

With no autopilot to help, if you let go of the stick, as maneuverable as the plane was, you could be upside down in less than a second. The roll rate for the A-4 was 720 degrees (two complete rolls) in a second, perhaps still the fastest roll rate, even today

Met up with some friends from *Coral Sea.* They told me we lost an F-8 on the O-Boat, Dave Matheny from VF-111. He was a good friend. Having had many drinks, and feeling as emotional as well, I went out on the back steps and cried for a couple of hours. Several different ladies from the wait staff tried to console me, but the collective losses we had, and having lost Dave my good friend and roommate, was just too much. Finally, I cried myself out and went back to finish drinking with my friends.

The pace of the operations since July was intense with almost daily strikes into the most heavily defended areas of North Vietnam. It seemed as if every day someone went down, sometimes rescued, sometimes KIA, and sometimes captured. It was over-whelming. Each of us tried to find a way to stay sane. Drinking be-came part of the attempt at sanity, but that wasn't enough. For my-self I made up my mind from the biblical saying, "Yea though I walk through the valley ...." from the 23rd Psalm, an excerpt with which most are familiar, but I ended mine with, "...I am the meanest 'M..F' in the valley." I was flying with an aggressive pilot, the Skipper, and I emulated his approach. I guess it worked.

The next day, Flight Operations at Cubi said I couldn't fly to Yankee by myself. I had just completed 1700 nautical miles by my-self and only had a short 900 left to get to Yankee.

I thought that was ridiculous; the squadron was counting on this plane. I submitted a flight plan to USAF Clark airbase, north of Cubi. In order to make it appear that this would be just a local trip, I did not get a full fuel load. The flight was approved; I went to Clark. Clark didn't care where I might go next; I was a Navy pilot, and they weren't responsible for me. I topped off all my tanks, filed a flight plan for a local trip and flew out to Yankee Station. I knew there would be a tanker available, and I could wait until the next recovery. I did need a splash of fuel, but I had made it back home. I am sure there is a statute of limitation on deceiving one's superi-ors, and breaking Navy rules.

It was back to the grind on 7 October. I was newly arrived and had the first Alpha to Hanoi. I was tracking at least 11 missiles and those where just the ones I could see. If you see the missile moving deflecting a reference point, you can disregard it; it is not tracking you. If it holds at a steady point, get ready to move at the last sec-ond because that sucker is tracking you! One of our VA-164 (Iron Hand) planes, our Shrike, radar-killer plane, flown by LT Dave Hodges, got hit by one of the missiles and went down without a chute.

The early afternoon Alpha to Haiphong was hot and heavy as always, not much fun, until we left and were headed home. Some-one called out "planes on the ground" at Kein An airfield.

Aircraft we left burning at Kien An Airfield. Author's photo.

I think every A-4 heading home put on the brakes and headed for the field. There were about seven An-2 planes on the ground, so we started strafing with our 20mm guns. I got mine, ran out of ammo, took a picture and left. They were all burning before the last plane left.

The AN-2 freighter like the ones we left burning.

Somehow, I think October got into a competition with September to see how much damage we sustained and how many losses we would have. My old friend Larry Cunningham was not satisfied getting shot down once, he had to do it all over again on the 9th. A helicopter from a destroyer picked him out of the water. Everyday someone on the ship was coming back with a hole in his airplane. A lot of bomb tape was used to patch holes quickly resulting in a lot of funny looking airplanes. It seemed as if we started bombing in the same area or same city a couple of days in a row with no reason or rationale; the enemy just loaded up and let us have it. October wasn't VA-164's month. On an Alpha to Haiphong on 18 October, LCDR John Barr was hit and exploded; there was no chute. I had a Walleye on board and my target was one of the bridges in Haiphong. We were trying to isolate the city by knocking down all the bridges.

A Walleye hit on a bridge in Haiphong. Author's photo.

I took a hit, but I didn't know it until I deployed my landing gear. Both main gears showed an "unsafe" in the indicator. My wingman checked, and he told me they were not down and locked.

I left the landing pattern, climbed up to around ten-thousand feet and performed several maneuvers to see if they would lock down. Nothing worked and they would not retract, either.

As a last ditch try, I dove toward the ground to pick up as much speed as I could. I pulled up hard and was able to get eight "Gs" (eight times the pull of gravity) onto the airplane. I then got a down and locked indication. After I landed, we could see the damage that prevented the normal operation of the gear.

On the 21st, I was night tanker. After covering the landings, I lost my airspeed indicator, my altimeter and my rate of climb indicator. At least the angle-of-attack indicator was working, and that one indicator would give me a proper landing speed. They sent up a replacement tanker to cover the landing aircraft.

Fate is inexorable, and it was our turn to start losing people. In Cubi one of our VA-4H A-3s was lost on takeoff. All four souls aboard were rescued.

I was the SDO on the 22nd. On the second Haiphong strike, LTJG James "Dools" Dooley was lost.

LTJG Jim "Dools" Dooley. Author's photo.

Dools was my ski instructor, an old roommate and a close friend. He always had this big smile on his face and was loved by all who knew him. I watched as the Skipper sat in front of me and cried at the loss of Dools.

I spent the next two days flying two Alpha missions each day to Haiphong.

The first strike was to a thermal power plant supplying electricity to Haiphong. As always, hot and heavy with missiles and flak. I was sixth in line to drop my bombs, and I saw the first several hit. They were producing plenty of electricity as lighting spikes ran across the ground with the hits. It was something to see. As I rolled off the target in an 80-degree bank, I was able to get several good photos of our hits.

Haiphong Thermal Power Plant. Photo by the author.

On the early afternoon flight of 24 October, my wingman, Skip Foulks, was hit and made it to the water. A helicopter picked him up, and in the early evening he was returned to the ship.

On 25 October, we were scheduled for three Alphas to the MiG base at Phuc Yen. It was some 12 miles north of Hanoi. This involved joint strikes by multiple carriers and the USAF. The base is tucked up against "Thud" ridge, so named because of the number of "Thuds" impacted there. I had the early and late afternoon missions. The first was a flak suppression mission. I took a bad hit from a missile. My damage consisted of buckling of the fuselage skin and multiple holes in the starboard fuselage.

Skip Foulks first return. Author's photo.

On the later flight, LT Jeff Krommenhoek, one of our replacement pilots, was on my left wing. We were rolling in on the revetment area where the MiGs were parked when I happened to look to my right. A missile was close and had me dead to rights. Out of

plain fright, I reflexively grabbed the stick (we tended to fly the A-4 with our fingers due to its sensitivity); the aircraft jumped a bit, and the missile went under me and right into Jeff.

He disappeared in this big fireball. I knew he didn't make it. I didn't have time to warn him or do much of anything else except roll in and deliver my weapons. The intensity of their defenses didn't allow for anything but action.

It was 26 October, the anniversary of the fire. I was the tanker on the early afternoon hop to Hanoi.

LTJG Chuck Rice, VF-162 was shot down and captured. LCDR John McCain was on his 20th mission flying on the Skipper's wing. They were bombing the thermal power plant in Hanoi. John got hit and ended up in the lake next to the city.

Hanoi, Vietnam. Photo by CDR Bryan Compton.

I most dreaded the thought of being a POW. Being single, my death would not have much of an effect on my survivors. But becoming a POW meant responsibilities to your fellow POWs, your shipmates and your country. I worried that I might not hold up to the stress of the torture that we knew was being inflicted. I might then do something to embarrass all.

After a couple more Alphas I got a break. We were short of flyable aircraft, and I was sent to Cubi to pick one up. I spent two days trying to drink the place dry. Happy-hour drinks were ten cents a pop. Give them ten dollars and, well ... you can do the math. Sharing was easy, because the next guy bought another hundred. The next day I returned to the ship. I flew on the wing of an A-3 replacement aircraft, because they still had that silly rule of no single aircraft flying out to Yankee.

I slept until 1600 and then briefed at 2330 for my night mission.

Starting your day at midnight makes for a long one, which was made even longer by the midnight launch being cancelled because the plane was down. My Halloween began with the 0400 launch and a second mission at 1130.

November began with two nighttime missions. We were back in the recce role and on the 12-hour flight schedule. I knew I had the SDO next day, but there would be no popcorn party. I was too damn tired.

I was not on the flight schedule, but others were. VA-164 lost another pilot, LTJG Freddie Knap. He went in with no chute and was listed as KIA.

A major storm with rough seas forced us to evacuate Yankee Station. The waves were just too big for safe operations.

CHAPTER TWENTY-FIVE

Yokosuka for R&R

We were now underway to Yokosuka naval base Japan. Although I had been to the city, I had not yet been to the Naval base.

When we got close, the squadron flew some of the airplanes to Atsugi for maintenance. Since I had duty, I did not get to fly.

When we arrived in Japan, we went alongside a dock, which made going ashore much easier. The next five days involved one duty day and four drinking days. I then got on a train with several of our guys and headed for Atsugi.

We needed to conduct some maintenance test flights as well as log some flying to keep everyone current. I organized a flight, to get a good picture of our airplanes flying a diamond formation over Mt. Fuji.

It is not easy to adjust the position of four jets flying formation while maintaining my own position to keep the shot looking like a proper diamond. If I changed position, the picture of what the formation looked like would alter.

I had to use my knees to fly the stick, my left hand on the throttle to keep the angle correct. My right hand held the camera and was used to check the composition of the picture. That hand also set the F-stop for light and advanced the film after shooting a photo.

Woody was the lead and kept a tight circle around the mountain which made my job even harder. The picture I took did not show the conical peak of Fuji, but it still came out well.

A VA-163 flight of four in diamond formation flying around Mount Fuji. Author's photo.

CHAPTER TWENTY-SIX

Fourth Line Period: 1967

On 16 November, some of our pilots left Atsugi for the O-Boat. They were flying freshly repaired airplanes.

Oriskany was returning to Yankee, but I was staying behind to get a plane from PAR. I'd then fly the same route as before: Okinawa, Philippines, then Yankee in the Gulf of Tonkin.

I did not have any idea when that might be. They were still working on the plane I was to pick up. While I was drinking, having fun, and getting some much-needed rest, my friends arrived at Yankee.

On 19 November, LT Ed Van Orden of VF-111 was killed after a bad cat shot.

Then the next day, LTJG Denny Earl, my touring guide in Japan, took a hit in the cockpit. He suffered major injuries to his legs, but he was able to land aboard using the barrier net. He was evacuated to the States.

These casualties made me feel guilty for not being there and contributing.

Then the weather was interfering with my test hop. When I finally got the thing airborne, it had a fuel leak, and it then went back into the shop.

The next day I took her up again. It was not the best A-4 I had ever flown, but I thought I could get it to Yankee. On the way to Naha, Okinawa I lost my radio. It wasn't really a big deal, because there was nobody to talk to anyway.

On the next day, with the nice tailwind that I had, I was making time. My speed across the ground was as if I were flying supersonic. So, I made it to the Philippines in good time. But the maintenance guys could not seem to fix the radio. On the 30th I caught the Carrier onboard Delivery (COD) aircraft back to the O-Boat. With that, the sun set on November.

On 1 December I was back on the recce schedule, and I flew two hops, enjoyed two good landings and logged my 100th and 101st mission in '67. I really could not believe I had made it this far.

The next day I was SDO—no flying, easy day. Back to flying two-a-day, on the 8th I was assigned two combat hops and one test hop.

We had encountered some bad weather, which resulted in a couple of weather recce flights. Then followed a Laos mission and another to Hanoi.

I had a problem with taking fuel on the way back to the ship and barely made it home.

I was given priority for landing over a couple of pilots who had just brought down a MiG-17: LT Dick Wyman of VF-162 and LTJG Chuck Nelson from the famous Ghostriders of VA-164.

Chuck took some amazing pictures while fighting the MiG, including the frames that included the MiG's demise: a remarkable feat.

For the next two days I flew two hops each day. Fatigue was setting in. Fortunately, we left the line the next day, 17 December, and I flew off to Cubi NAS. It had been a short on-the-line period.

CHAPTER TWENTY-SEVEN

R&R in Hong Kong

W e stayed in Cubi for several days and then left for Hong Kong to arrive on the 24th.

This was my favorite R&R city. We weren't scheduled to return to Yankee until 31 December, so we had Christmas Day off.

With all this time for shopping and dining in Hong Kong, I was sure I would go broke by the time we left.

I had Shore Patrol duty first night in that port, and I parlayed that into some nice times.

There was a neat floating city called Aberdeen, which was a short boat trip away.

That city consisted of every kind of boat you could imagine, all tied together. You were expected walk between them, and those living on these vessels would try to sell us various sea creatures for eating.

Several of the bigger boats, the Chinese sailing junks, were restaurants. The food served was delicious: nice and fresh, a remarkably interesting place to visit.

Hong Kong was great, and I was, as feared, broke. So, back to war.

CHAPTER TWENTY-EIGHT

Final '67 On Line Period

I had a mission on New Year's Eve, a good hop with one of our new pilots, LTJG Scotty "Fat Boy" Mitchell. He was not fat; remember we did not get to choose our call signs. We encountered only 37mm guns and we got our bombs on the target.

Good-bye, 1967.

New Year's Day for 1968 began at the 0430 brief for my first hop. No moon, black-as-hell night catapult shot with no visible horizon. Not a comfortable feeling.

The only good thing I can say about night flying is that they do not shoot accurately, because they can't see you. It was more like watching fireworks on the Fourth of July.

My buddy LTJG George Schindlar of VA-164 ejected on the way to Chu Lai.

He was rescued thankfully. We also lost a reconnaissance flight, a RA-3, to flak with three souls on board. Not a great start to 1968.

The next day was not much better.

I led two good hops for us. However, that day LTJG Craig Taylor of VF-111, escorting one of the RF-8 photo birds, went down and didn't survive.

My hops the next day started with a night tanker flight followed by an Alpha to Hai Doung. My first hop on 3 January was cancelled; my aircraft was broken. The second mission was another Alpha back to Hai Doung.

LTJG Rich Minnich of VF-162 was hit by a missile and did not survive. My plane sustained some 37mm damage to the left side of the fuselage, the tail and the horizontal stabilizer.

The year 1968 did not seem to be any better than 1967. We continued to lose pilots and get airplanes shot up.

The night of the 5th, LT "Step" Landroth was leading a section in RP IV, with LTJG "Skip" Foulks as his wingman. Skip rolled in on the target and flew into the ground.

"Skip" Foulks. Author's photo.

There was shooting, but Step did not know if "Skip" had been hit. I was leading another section in the next launch and spent time looking for "Skip."

There was no radio contact with him, and he was declared KIA. "Skip" was our youngest pilot, our baby and a fine young man. He was married about two weeks before we left the States, thus leaving another young widow. To lose him so close to going home was hard on all of us.

I was duty officer on the 6th and flew two missions on the 7th. Bad weather cancelled our hops on the 8th. I flew twice on the 9th and was duty officer the next day. I was scheduled for two hops to Laos on the 11th, our last day this cruise. Both hops were successful missions, but on the second flight, LCDR Deny Weichman of VA-164 had been hit and ejected. He was picked up by a helicopter.

That was our last loss on this tour.

Combat Photos

*Above is a half-Alpha strike inbound to target,
and below is a Division of VA-163 A-4s inbound.*

This is a SAM site near Hanoi photographed at close range. In the photo below is an emplacement of 85-mm guns. These guns were almost always guided by radar.

Above, white puffs of 37mm flak at Hai Dong.
and below, a burning storage area near Haiphong.
Both are photos by the author.

Above, a rare occurrence: rail cars left out as daylight targets.
Below, trucks are burning in the center of this photo. Author's photos.

Phuc Yen MiG airfield as seen by the author inbound to this target.
Below is the runway at the base after the strike.
Both photos by the author.

MiG revetments at Phuc Yen. Author's photo above.
A Walleye glide bomb exploded in this Hanger (photo below)
This photo was shot by LTJG Fritz Schroeder who dropped the weapon.

As the A-4 is shot off the ship in a catapult shot, the stress temporarily wrinkles the skin on the fuselage (visible behind the intake inlet). Below a Saints A-4 is almost clear of the bow. Author photo.

CHAPTER TWENTY-NINE

Yokosuka and Then Home

W e headed back to Yokosuka Japan. From there the Air Wing's pilots would fly home on chartered civilian airliners.

We were to leave from a USAF Air base in Tachikawa, about 30 miles from the Naval base at Yokosuka. There the ship would be readied for the long crossing to the States.

While we were enroute to Japan, North Korea captured the *USS Pueblo*. Washington decided to send *Oriskany* to the waters just off Korea. We all were stunned. This was like the straw that broke the camel's back.

Fortunately, the Navy came to our aid, informing Washington that because of our losses, we would return to CONUS (Continental United States).

This pleased us to no end.

Oriskany tied up alongside the dock in Yokosuka, and we pilots took a bus to Tachikawa, the big USAF base that is now called Fussa Air Base, for our flight home.

A big party was planned for the officer's club. The club was reluctant to rent us the space for our party, giving the excuse that Navy pilots were too rowdy.

It was a very elegant club, but money is money after all.

Afterward, I am sure they regretted their decision.

The food was buffet style. But we weren't interested in food as much as drinking. It quickly escalated to burner lights, and I ended up in sumo matches against various characters from all the squadrons. This was not a hard thing for me to do, since I wrestled in high school and college. For luck I threw salt over my shoulder the way I had seen the real sumo wrestlers do. We did break a few tables, but I didn't lose a match.

CDR Span the executive officer of VA-164 was the bull fighter, CDR "Fast Eddy" Lighter our executive officer the bull.

The next thing we knew, both went through the door into the formal dining room, right into the table of a couple having a nice dinner.

That was the last straw for the USAF. They threw us all out.

Hey, we didn't mind. There was enough money in the kitty to pay for damages, and we were leaving the next day for home. I think it might have been World Airways that flew us back to San Francisco, the city of our departure.

CHAPTER THIRTY

1968 and Home

Step, Fritz, and I had some good friends, Gary and Linda White, and they greeted us as we cleared customs. Gary and Step had gone to USC together, fraternity brothers. I had not planned on going to either of my parent's homes, and I was invited by Gary to stay with them. We went to a hotel to relax, and then in his nice Beech Bonanza, Gary flew Linda and me back to their home in Three Rivers, California.

Three Rivers was relatively close to Lemoore, our base, so his restaurant, The White Horse Inn, had for my squadron become our home away from home.

Good times were enjoyed there before we left, and now that we were back, more fine times were ahead.

Three Rivers had a small, one direction only landing strip. Gary and I went to Hanford, picked the N3N up and flew her back. The strip was in a valley, you flew into the closed end of the valley, turned to land on the strip. If you had to abandon the landing, you went straight ahead until reaching the river, turn down the river and climb over the lake to get altitude to fly back for another landing, or leave the area. A fun place to visit.

*Gary in the back seat of Ken's N3N and the author in front
in this photo shot by Linda White.*

The first order of business was to go skiing. Gary, Linda, Step, and I went to Squaw Valley.

The new plastic ski boots were the hot item, so to speak.

Step bought some new Lange boots. They hurt his feet, but he had heard that he should put them in the oven, heat them up, and then put them onto his feet to make them conform.

He did this, but when he put them on, they were too hot. He headed out the door and jumped into a mound of snow, disappearing as his boots melted the snow.

We were laughing so hard we thought we might die.

The next few days were hard, the people there knew we were military, calling us all kinds of names, throwing frozen, iced snowballs at us, and keying our cars which included Gary's—and he wasn't even in the military.

We had to leave early; it was definitely an eye opener. We quickly found out we couldn't leave the base in our uniforms.

Most of us didn't want to leave the base, unless it was to go to Gary's White Horse Inn. Unwanted, abandoned in our own country: not a good feeling, especially considering the friends we had lost.

CHAPTER THIRTY-ONE

Squadron Refit

We were changing airwings and ships. The last break from combat did not permit sufficient time for *Oriskany* to get the much-needed repairs, some of which were major.

Now that we were limiting our bombing of North Vietnam to the area below the 20th parallel, the Navy could take the time to repair her.

We were reassigned to Air Wing 21, and we would be based on *USS Hancock*, CVA-19, a ship older than the O-Boat. The squadron was being expanded to 18 pilots; nine were new to the squadron and combat. I was the longest serving Saint, and Goose was a close second. We were not the most senior pilots by rank but our new Skipper, "Fast Eddy" was counting on us to lead the training of our new pilots.

CDR Ed "Fast Eddy" Lighter. Author photo.

It was a demanding role with much strategic, functional, and practical material to cover. More than once, I slept in the hangar ready-room, getting in late from night bombing practice, and then doing something as simple as following one of our guys on his nuclear qualification.

As the leader for the night bombing, I had the newest pilots, those with the least flying time. With three of them on my wing, we headed to Fallon, Nevada, where the targets were.

I carried the flares and dropped them for their bombing targets. In addition, I tried to keep track of their accuracy. Following the bombing runs, the pilots rendezvoused with me and we headed home.

Night rendezvous were dangerous. The lead pilot flew a wide circle maintaining a 30-degree bank. The pilot joining on the lead flew on the inside of the circle, banking his airplane to fly a wider circle; when the two circles intersected, they were joined and "on my wing," so to speak.

It's an efficient way to join at a defined spot in space and is known as the rendezvous circle. At night the pilot attempting the rendezvous had only a wingtip light as a guide.

Multiple planes forming on a leader made it especially dangerous. As a pilot joined on my inside of the circle wing position, he then moved to the outside of the circle, which elevated him on my raised wing.

The next pilot joining would first settle on the inside of the circle and then move to the outside of the number two airplane. They each flew off the wingtip light and, because of their raised position, could not see the next pilot rendezvousing. Sometimes the rendezvousing pilot closed too fast. When the pilot realized this, he increased his bank angle, putting some additional "G" on the airplane, trying to match the circle I was flying. When he increased the bank, he would lose sight of me and his closure rate could still be too fast meaning he might hit me. I would have to climb quickly and hope those on my wing would react and climb with me. I also hoped the rendezvousing pilot would slide underneath me. Then he had to figure out how to join the formation, not an easy task since he was now on the outside of the circle.

To help him recover, I would usually roll wings level so we would fly straight-and-level while he tried to rejoin. This was a scary situation that happened more than once. It is a hard maneuver to do at night and do it safely.

Chasing the nuclear qualifying pilot in the morning after the night flying was almost as dangerous. I trailed the qualifier, but stepped up a few feet so I could watch where he was headed and keep track of his timing. He flew 50 feet above the ground at 360 knots; I was at about 70 feet.

Since I was usually tired, I tended to drop off for a second or two (now known as micro-naps), awaken with a start with my heart pounding, with the realization that my life depended on remaining alert. Then it would happen again a few more miles down the road. Our schedules had us working around 14 hours a day, day after day; everyone was tired.

The Navy had come up with a new A-4 called the TA-4J, a two-seat, tandem airplane to be used as a pilot trainer. Since our aircraft were beat up and needed to be repaired, we were assigned several of these planes. The plane had all the bombing stations we had on the "Echoes" we were flying, so the training didn't get interrupted. The tandem seating gave us the opportunity to get our hard-working enlisted sailors airborne. All those who wanted to fly were given the necessary training to allow them to fly with us.

To a man, even those subject to motion or airsickness, they enjoyed the opportunity to see what our mission consisted of. At our reunions, they still talked about their flights and how they enjoyed it. This helped our squadron morale. The days were long and hard with little personal time off. I was glad we had this opportunity; our crews deserved the best treatment that we could offer.

We were quickly approaching our deployment time to Fallon, where the airwing practiced the Alpha-strike method of flying and had a chance for bonding into a working unit. On this cruise, we wouldn't have "Spads" in our airwing. They had been replaced by a third A-4 squadron, flying the new "Foxtrot" model of the A-4.

The Foxtrot had small improvements over the Echo but still carried the same ordnance. Our F-8 squadrons were VF-211 and VF-24. The airwing was about the same as our old Air Wing 16 but with new faces and a new ship.

Early in the training I had a fun day, a practice rescue of a sham downing of a pilot (me). On the mission, I made the radio call that I had been hit, that I was going down. It seemed that the organizers failed to include the safety teams in the details of the drill planning. They thought it was a real downing, so the practice was called off. I had already returned and landed by the time they had launched a helicopter to find me. FUBAR again.

Our next exercise took us aboard the "Hanna," as the *USS Hancock* was called, to practice working off the ship and getting landing practice. The time was flying by, and we would be deploying shortly.

The constant moving from one base to another, to the ship and then back to Lemoore was getting a bit old. I was able finally to take some leave and returned to Michigan and Florida to see my family. I flew TWA on my way back to the base; the captain saw me boarding with a marine vet and had the flight attendant move us up to first class.

This was the first time either of us had been shown any appreciation since our return to the states. The flight attendant informed us the captain was a WWII vet. We both shook his hand as we left the plane.

CHAPTER THIRTY-TWO

Getting Underway: 1968

The second week in July we flew to NAS Alameda to start loading our planes on the Hanna for our upcoming deployment. As my last shore stop prior to boarding, I went to Heinold's First and Last Chance saloon for my last drink ashore. It brought me good luck the prior year; I hoped it would be lucky this year.

As the ship left the dock on 18 July, many friends were there to bid me *adieu*. We passed under the Golden Gate Bridge, again to an uncertain future. My thoughts were of those we lost and those who would never have the return passage under the bridge.

It really is quite a sight despite the uneasiness it created. I just had to get accustomed to the idea of living on a day-to-day basis. It always took time for that to sink in; but once it did, I felt better. The constant pressure is tiring and being one of the more experienced pilots brought more responsibility. Well, at least we would be docking in Hawaii in a few days, and it was always a nice place to visit.

I was the SDO on the 19th. I was responsible to get the ready-room organized and make it our new home for the next seven months. The next day I met with the riggers to get my combat harness prepped. I still planned on flying in Marine fatigues; the new, green Nomex flight suits were made of fire-retardant material, but they didn't fit well and were very scratchy.

We all lined up on the evening of the 20th so our new flight surgeon could give us our four big shots to protect us from a variety of diseases if we were taken prisoner. It would take more than a shot of medicine, but at least they were trying. We weren't permitted to wear rings, our own watches or anything personal. I didn't wear any jewelry, so it was not a big problem for me.

I awoke the next morning and was very sore from those damn shots. Some members of the squadron took a test flight with some of our new LCDR leaders. They didn't have any combat experience, and it was very apparent with their lack of organization. The Skipper promoted me to a combat-division leader. I hoped when we got on the line, I could do my own thing and not rely on our new, inexperienced leaders.

In order to create some deck space for newbie training, I was assigned to be one of four pilots to fly aircraft from Hawaii to the Philippines. I was the leader of the group, and it was nice to have some company over a long expanse of nothing but water. My roommate was Griff "Baron" Sexton. We roomed together ashore so it was a natural fit for the ship. We had a good time together. He was one of the other pilots assigned to be with me on the Trans-Pac, so we could get in trouble together.

But before all that came to pass, I had to have time to get sick from those damn shots; I felt like crap most of the day. Fortunately, I wasn't assigned to fly and wasn't sure I could have if I were scheduled. I got my sea legs back and got used to being back on the ship.

The morning of 23 July found me feeling much better. I was scheduled for a night hop and felt well enough to do it. I had problems with the instrument lighting; it wouldn't dim. I spent a much of the time with the lights off. I have always been sensitive to light. I hooked the flashlight with the red lens to my harness so I could see some of the panel display. It was black as Hades with no differentiation between the black night and the black water. I got down OK with a good landing grade. The most important thing is: you can be scared; you just can't admit to it. You have to look good, even if you die. The Navy pilot's prayer is, "Please God, don't let me look bad."

We arrived at Pearl on the 24th and had shore leave. We had a fun day off the boat followed by some good drinking in the evening. The Army had a nice base on Oahu with great beaches and was the only inexpensive place on the Island. Their drinks were almost as inexpensive as those at our Navy bases. We were scheduled for our operational readiness inspection (ORI) on the next day to make certain that we could be released to Vietnam.

The ship left port in the morning to hold the ORI in the waters off Hawaii. We had some practice hops which included a practice Alpha strike. I got some good pictures and that pleased our new CAG, Captain Hal Terry. CAGs used to be Commanders (O-5) but now they were Captains (O-6). We were not sure of the reason for that, but that was above my pay grade. I was promoted to Lieutenant (O-3, comparable to captain in the Army, Air Force and Marines) in May. I d wear double silver bars.

On the next day, we simulated being a midnight-to-noon carrier. I had a 0130 launch. As I sat and listened to the intelligence briefing, I got some bad news. LCDR Bill Rankin was lost on the midnight launch.

I at first thought this was an exercise for the ORI, but the XO confirmed his death. Bill didn't rotate his plane off the cat and subsequently didn't establish a climb. He lost altitude until he was flying on "ground effect," an aerodynamic event where the compression of air underneath the airplane will keep it from getting any lower. When Bill raised the flaps, as would be expected, that changed the aerodynamics, and he flew into the water creating a big fireball.

I felt then, and still feel today, that I was responsible for his loss. At lunch the day before we left port for the ORI, Bill explained to me that he felt his skills were behind the speed of things happening with the A-4, especially just off the cat.

Bill had flown the S-2 Tracker, a seagoing, anti-submarine plane with a top speed of 140 knots, which was the speed reached at the end of the cat stroke.

The fleet was short of jet pilots. Jeff Krommenhoek, my wingman that was lost in '67, had also been an S-2 pilot. It made it difficult for him to fly and keep his lookout as sharp as it should have been.

LCDR Bill Rankin. Author photo.

Now it was Bill who was having to fly and think at a much higher speed. I felt that with time and experience he would catch up. I should have gone to the Skipper and told him to keep Bill off the night schedule until he got more experience. I didn't do that.

I didn't want to hurt Bill's career. I was wrong.

Bill confided in me about this problem, and I should have suggested to him to keep off the night schedule. I also blamed pri-fly; the observers up there were supposed to watch the launch, and if they saw a plane not climbing, tell the pilot to rotate.

If the A-4 had a full load, you had to rotate to the stall and then back off to get her climbing. I had given that tip to Bill, but I didn't think through the problem enough.

The next day we flew the planes off to Barbers Point Naval Air Station. After the ship docked, we went aboard for a memorial service for Bill. The next couple days we had a great time at the beach, sailing through the surf with the outrigger canoes. What a way to enjoy our time. Dick "Greasy" Harriss had his girlfriend come over; they were to be married on the next day.

CHAPTER THIRTY-THREE

Trans-Pac

On 31 July I would be flying a long trip, but not as long as Grease's walk down the aisle. We gave them a proper Navy wedding including the crossed swords.

Then Griff and I got out to Barbers Point to begin the Trans-Pac. I was leading a four-plane to Wake Island, a five-hour, forty-minute flight, 2190 nautical miles of blue pacific water. We had an A-3 "Whale" tanker to lead us out of Hawaii and top off our tanks after about two hours of flying. The pilot told us that Wake was "That way." Although we were sure he thought it was funny, with wide expanses of water everywhere, it wasn't all that humorous.

We flew north of Johnston Atoll, a top-secret, nuclear-test facility with a landing field, but we were not allowed to stop there and re-fuel. Some three hundred miles past Johnston, Griff had fuel problems and couldn't get fuel out of the external tanks. We wouldn't make Wake. I ordered the other two to continue to Wake.

Griff and I returned to Johnston; I had to declare an emergency, so they had to let us land. After we landed, they wouldn't let us get out of the cockpit, but they relented to permit us out to pee. They held guns on us, as we lined up against a wall to empty our bladders. Thankfully, they let us leave; I wasn't looking forward to spending a few years in jail.

We made it across the international date line; it was now August. We landed at Wake after seven, tiring hours of flying 2600 nautical miles, which was my personal record in an A-4 cockpit. My butt was sore. Griff had an electrical problem with his airplane. I sent the other two on to Guam, while we waited for parts. A maintenance crew worked hard on the plane and fixed the problem. I called the Navy supply main man, Capt. Laws, and cancelled our request for a generator. We started drinking early, and the prices were good.

The next morning, we left for Guam, a short 1250 nautical miles of open water; fortunately, we didn't have a problem, which was quite unbelievable. Griff and I caught up with our compatriots in Gaum. I gave a quick brief to the line crew, who were unfamiliar with the A-4, on how to refuel the aircraft. We went to lunch, which was a big mistake.

We had planned for a launch with all four of us heading to Cubi Point. Apparently, my briefing wasn't as clear as I had hoped, regarding some details of the refueling process. I couldn't get the gas cap off my center-line, fuel tank to check the fuel. When I finally got it loose, it blew off because they had pressure-fueled it, which was something I said not to do.

Trapped air kept the cap from coming off and didn't allow for the tank to fill completely. We manually filled the tank and reinstalled the fuel cap, but I didn't notice that a rubber seal was missing. We didn't want to run out of daylight, so we had to hurry to get launched.

We had two problems right after launch. I was leaking fuel and getting heavy fumes in the cockpit. Griff was unable to raise his gear. The line crew missed one of the gear pins. They would show you a handful of gear pins, giving the impression that the pins had been removed, but it was hard to tell if they had removed all three or not. "Or not" was what I found later as I slid underneath his plane to look at the gear.

I ordered our compatriots to get to Cubi. We returned to Guam and landed. We drank at the club as usual, trying to solve the world's problems, but we didn't have any good answers.

The next morning, we flew our A-4s, along with an A-3 from the *USS America*, VAH-10, to Cubi Point.

To be accompanied by an aircraft capable of giving us some fuel was a nice break for a 1,450 nautical mile flight. As we entered the pattern at Cubi, we flew over the *USS America*. She was twice as wide as either the O-Boat or Hanna.

I got out of the cockpit having completed, a 5,600 nautical-mile trip over the blue Pacific Ocean with no land beneath. It was a hell of a trip in a single-seat aircraft.

CHAPTER THIRTY-FOUR

Yokosuka Again

Griff and I were staying at the Cubi BOQ and met with several of our friends from training days: John Ryan and Peyton Dobbins, both flying F-4s off the *USS America*, and Strom Evans flying off the *USS Intrepid*.

That night we went to the officers' club at Subic Bay, the fancy one. We had a grand time and behaved ourselves around all the black-shoe officers. When it came time to leave, we called for a taxi. It was the only form of transportation on the base. I thought it criminal, as sailors on a US Navy base, that we had to pay to get around on the base. As if getting shot at wasn't enough. The cabs came in two sizes: three or five passengers. We had asked for a large car and got the small one. We started yelling at the driver and pounding on his car. Someone called shore patrol; we heard the siren coming up the hill, and we melted into the jungle. The last I saw of Peyton, he was hanging by one arm from a tree, sounding like a monkey. Eventually Griff and I made it back to the Cubi BOQ, and I presume they made it back to their ships.

We spent 5 August trying to catch an Air Force C-141 ride to Yokota. The Hanna was sailing to Yokosuka from Hawaii and Yokota was the closest Air Force base. Finally, at 0100 on the 6th, we caught a flight thinking we were on our way at last, but we were wrong. It had a mechanical problem and had to divert to Clark Air Base. There weren't rooms for us at the BOQ, so we rented a hotel room in Angeles City. I have been in some seedy hotels, and this was a nasty room without air-conditioning. We caught a flight out of Clark the next day and arrived in Yokota around 1800. We ended up at the officers' club and tried to drink Japan dry. We didn't succeed.

I spent the next day trying to get some rest and recover from all that flying across the world's largest ocean. I took in a hotsy bath, which relieved my sore butt. A good night's sleep also helped a lot. We finally returned to our ship on the 8th, via helicopter, courtesy of the commander of Air Wing 21, Captain Hal Terry. I borrowed some money from Step, went ashore in Yokosuka and bought some more camera accessories. I ended the day at the club on base and used my hotsy bath routine from the previous year, to get drunk twice. I returned to the ship and a deep sleep.

The next day Goose, Fritz and I rented a 28-foot, Dragon sailboat. Man, that thing could fly. A smooth sailing ship with a beautiful design and nice wood trim. I would have liked to have owned one, but that was not possible then. We ended the day with a nice meal in town, then went back to the big ship.

The base at Yokosuka had a nice gym. On the 10th I played handball with Step, but Step smoked like a chimney; he didn't last long. The loss must have had an effect on him because he quit smoking that morning and has never smoked since. It was easy to smoke in the military. Cigarettes were cheap with no tax on them, and you could get them anywhere. Step showed great will power to stop. I played some basketball and looked for more electronic toys. We ended the day with a great sukiyaki dinner accompanied by some drinking, of course.

We departed Yokosuka 11 August for Subic Bay and Cubi Point. We sailed into a typhoon, which curtailed any flying. I helped plan a practice Alpha strike with the XO, CDR. Ed Shropshire. Commander "Fast Eddy" Lighter was our new Skipper. I had a good relationship with Fast Eddy and was appointed as one of the division leaders for that cruise. That was a nice appointment for a junior Lieutenant. I had been promoted before we left the states and I was now assistant, maintenance division officer. It was a great job, but I missed my line division guys.

CHAPTER THIRTY-FIVE

Underway to Cubi

The seas were a bit rough off the Japanese coast on 12 August, but it didn't cancel our need to fly for currency with ship operations.

LTJG. Griff "Baron" Sexton, my roomie back in Lemoore, was now my roomie on ship. He was flying on my wing for a quick flight with a return to the ship for landing.

I landed first. Griff had a problem when his port main gear hit the round down (the rear part of the flight deck) and damaged his hook.

I heard the radio call to him from the LSO and knew he would have to fly into the barricade for his landing. I quickly moved to the crow's nest, the deck on the side of the ship's radar antenna housing. I had my camera at the ready.

I'm sure the crew was wondering why a pilot would want to sit there and watch landings, but they didn't wonder much after the call to rig the barricade. I then had plenty of company, but I was in a great position to get good photos. Griff did a good job into the barricade, but it trashed another airplane for us.

LTJG Griff "Baron" Sexton in the barricade. Author's photos.

Not yet on the line and we were down two airplanes, one pilot and the ship lost a sailor overboard. Not such a great start.

On the 13th we were off the coast of Okinawa and I was scheduled for two hops plus a physical. I passed my physical and flew on the wing of LCDR. Dean "Dynamite" Cramer: one day hop, the other a night trap. For the day landing, the LSO had to use a manual ball since the deck was moving too much for the Fresnel lens. The LSO had a handle to manually move the ball to correct for the deck movement and kept the pilot on the glide path he wanted the pilot to fly. If the deck was moving too much when you got in close, he waved you off and you got back in line to try again. By night the seas had calmed, so that was helpful. I had two good landings, which was a good start to winning some money. Nothing felt quite as good as winning money. I felt extremely comfortable around the boat, and that was nice feeling to have.

We were now off the coast of the Philippines on 14 August, and I had the duty so no flying to Cubi for me. The planes left for a good wash; they had gotten plenty of salt water because of the heavy seas we had been sailing.

We spent the 15th and 16th in port at Cubi. Griff's airplane was off-loaded since it needed major repairs to make it flight-worthy. We left Cubi on the 17th, but the ship had some equipment issues so our arrival at Yankee Station was delayed. I had been scheduled for two flights but neither got off the ship. She really was a tired, old boat. We hoped things would improve in the days to come. The next day was landing practice for all the new pilots: launch, land, repeat. The old-timers just had to sit around, bored to tears. We tried critiquing some of the landings with bets on what the next guy would do. That wasn't much better than being bored, but it kept us awake. I got airborne with Fat Boy. We found a couple of F-8s willing to dog-fight. We won the first fight and lost the second. At least we gave them some competition. It was fun pulling all those Gs.

My night flight was cancelled as an F-8 went down due to fuel starvation. The pilot was picked up by a destroyer. The destroyer guys were a good bunch. Since my '66 cruise, they picked up many of us. It was nice to know they had our backs. They didn't report me for the fun I had with them on occasion. When I had some extra fuel that I could waste, not having a Charlie time for landing, I would get down level with the command deck. I flew at the ship and played chicken. When I first started this, the ship would always make a quick turn; then they got serious and stayed on course. I think it evened out between it turning at the last second or my slight climb to give them a close flyover. I think they enjoyed the game.

In another playful moment I led myself and my wingman to climb to a high altitude and then descended toward Hainan Island, a Chinese island to the east of Haiphong. I listened for an announcement from our electronic, eavesdropping aircraft that they were launching MiGs. We continued our high-speed descent and turned out to sea and international water. I did that twice before I was ordered not to do that again. What a shame, it was fun to go that fast and get them to waste launching airplanes. It certainly wasn't boring.

The repairs on the Hanna were completed on 20 August and we headed for Yankee Station. We had bad weather from a typhoon so I completed only one hop; the pitching deck was outside the limits. That's kind of a funny statement since I still remember our '67 cruise. I guess that sea was inside the limits of what losing pilots and planes were. At least I got another "OK" trap, so I was at the top of the landing board. I wouldn't keep all that money for myself. I would share with my buds because we are all in this crap together.

I planned to use some of those special lenses I purchased in Japan. I also wanted to try some black and white exposures as well. To get good results you needed to think differently; I wasn't sure I was that talented. At least it kept me busy. I also found a new reading challenge: I laid out three books, read both facing pages from each book, turned pages and repeated the process. It was a challenge to keep up with all the stories. It kept me occupied enough to not get into trouble flying at things I shouldn't. But it was fun playing with that train over in the Kern River valley. It was a bright moonlit night, and I could see the train tracks clearly. I saw a train ahead of me, heading toward me; his single headlight wobbled a bit so the engineer could see the track clearly. I slowed down, put my gear and flaps down and tried to taxi on the rails heading toward the train. The A-4 had a taxi light on the nose gear that we never really used. I turned it on and the hit the rudder to move the light like his headlight. I guess he figured there was a train heading toward him, so he applied the brakes. There were a lot of sparks flying from those wheels. I pulled up my gear and made a climbing turn away from the train, so I don't think he knew I had been there. It's a good thing they needed pilots to fly in combat. If I was in the peacetime Navy, I'd have been in jail for a long time.

PART V

A Third Combat Go

Never tell people how to do things. Tell them what to do and they will surprise you with their ingenuity.

George S. Patton Jr.

The author ready to launch.

CHAPTER THIRTY-SIX

Rules of the War: 1968

We spent two days being bored, sitting through the various briefings about how the war was going and how things had changed since our last deployment.

Before we left the States, President Johnson announced a bombing halt for the area of North Vietnam above the 20-degrees-north latitude line.

The Navy was now responsible for the old Route Pack II and Route Pack III regions extending RP III to 20-degrees north. The vibes I was getting from the air wing was that we would fly Alpha strike missions into these areas.

Having flown in both those RPs since '66, I knew there was nothing there that required a major strike. But senior officers needed to have big strikes in their resume to move ahead.

In '66 and '67 we worked these areas with a section of A-4s. (two planes). There remained no real threat in these areas. Since we were no longer going to Hanoi, the North Vietnamese moved some missiles and guns into the areas we would be working.

Might as well make it as uncomfortable for us as they could. I believed it was crazy to continue to bomb these areas. There was nothing there that hadn't been bombed into oblivion. There was nothing there but holes in the earth and dirt moved from one hole to the other.

We should have cut back the number of carriers and helped our troops fighting on the ground in the south.

Nobody would listen to me anyway, so let's just get on with it.

CHAPTER THIRTY-SEVEN

First On Line Period: 1968

It was 23 August 1968 and I was finally back in the war. I took my wingman, LTJG Earl "Jello Man" Groff on his first combat mission.

We had a new tool in defending against radar-controlled guns: a chaff dispenser. Chaff consists of small strips of aluminum that reflect radar waves. While enroute to the beach, each pilot would launch a tube of chaff. The other pilot would observe if the chaff deployed and inform the pilot whether his system was working. That way each aircraft would have some protection against radar tracking. When I checked mine, Jello reported it worked. The chaff expanded quickly. To Jello, it looked like a white fluffy cloud. This led to a funny, but possible deadly, confusion later in our flight.

On this flight, I had a few firsts for the squadron this new line period: first to find a truck, first to miss a truck and first to get shot at.

I started our recce hop in the southern part of the old RPII below Vinh working along old Route 1, the highway along the coast from the DMZ to Haiphong. As we progressed, Jello asked if I was deploying chaff. I responded that I was not. I found a truck and asked Jello if he had it in sight. He replied that he did not. I climbed up to 10,000 feet and rolled in on the target. I misjudged the wind and missed the truck, which then moved quickly off the road and into the jungle. I missed one target, but we finally found some intact bridges, brought them down and returned to the *Hanna*.

I got my "OK 3(wire)" (the three wire is the target wire) which made me happy. I was still in the lead to win the landing pot.

During the debrief, I asked Jello why he thought I was dispensing chaff. He replied he saw these white puffs behind my airplane as we started north on Route 1.

I explained to him that was a 37mm gun tracking me and the white puffs were the exploding rounds. I was being shot at, but he didn't recognize what was happening. I may have become a little excited, but he never forgot that lesson.

Our second mission worked again on Routes 1 and 15 north of Vinh. We didn't find any truck movements but put craters in a road and dropped on some bypass bridges for another easy mission. A good way to get started. I got another "OK 3" so I was still at the top of the landing board. I felt that money burning a hole in my pocket.

Later that night we had an oiler/supply ship come alongside. It was a black night illuminated with red lighting everywhere: an impressive sight. Fuel was transferred, bombs came aboard along with food and other supplies. The black-shoe navy was very impressive that night. They got the job done with no losses.

The next morning, I led the XO on a Rescue Combat Air Patrol "RESCAP" mission, which we now were now flying almost every launch. We were to be the quick-on-station aircraft in case a pilot was on the ground or in the water. The aircraft were loaded with two, 500-hundred-pound bombs, one each on the outboard wing station; each inboard station had a 300-gallon fuel tank; a Hughes Mark IV external gun pod was mounted on the centerline. The gun pod was a point and shoot weapon that could fire 4,000 rounds per minute, but it was limited to a four-second burst. The pod was a totally self-contained unit with 750, 22mm rounds. A nice weapon for a RESCAP mission. After the other aircraft were feet wet, we went in, found a couple of barges, dropped our bombs on them, sunk one and strafed the other with our gun pods. Good hits with the guns on the second barge, but it was not on fire and did not sink.

On the second hop with Jello, we continued his education about North Vietnam. We started up by Than Hoa, showed him the infamous bridge and then worked south on Route 1. We found some rail cars that looked like they were in good condition, so we bombed them, put some more holes in the road and came home. It wasn't an exciting day, but we came home safely and I had two landings good enough to stay at the top the landing board.

On the morning of 25 August, I went with the XO as his second-division lead on what was considered an Alpha strike. We had three A-4 squadrons, each contributing eight A-4s, combined with our F-8s. We had more airplanes on the strike than last year. Most of them now flying had little combat experience. I couldn't believe how much all these airplanes were moving around. It was chaotic, and we were still over water. I moved my division way out to the right and just flew without moving around to be safe. The target was assigned by Washington and was supposed to be a transship-ment point, but it was just open dirt piles in reality. I rolled my di-vision in last and got some good hits; but overall, there was no fire and no indication we hit anything except the ground.

My second hop also was with the XO. He was very calm, easy going and knew how to fly. We found a truck on Route 1, which neither of us could believe; we were configured as RESCAP aircraft. We only hit it with our 20mm bullets, which did not set it on fire. At least it couldn't be driven. Another two good landings, so that made my day.

I was underutilized on 26 August. I started as duty officer, flew a tanker hop and sat through two briefings as a spare pilot. Just like a spare anything, I sat idle. So far, on that deployment, I felt that my knowledge and experience were irrelevant.

Irrespective of intel obtained by the pilots flying various mis-sions, some unknown person or persons in Washington, with no experience of what we do or see, determined the targets. Had they asked us, we could have provided pictures that showed there was no target, just holes in the ground.

No targets, just holes in the earth. Author photo.

When I first joined the squadron in August of 1966, two A-4s were assigned to a RP with no other aircraft. The lead pilot could change the ordnance to fit the mission assigned. We were effective and didn't have excessive losses. With the target limitations as of mid-1968, the Navy could have trained us to work with troops and move at least one carrier back to Dixie to provide air support for our ground troops. That could have saved some lives instead of making new holes in the terrain.

The next morning, I was assigned to fly one of our broken birds to Cubi. I had a nice, relaxing flight despite contending with a lot of weather. I checked in at the BOQ, had a nice sleep and then was off to the club for dinner and drinks.

I was ready on 28 August to return to Yankee Station, but that bugaboo rule of needing a second airplane to fly from Cubi to Yankee reared its ugly head once more. I could fly by myself from Yankee Station to Cubi but not back. They wouldn't fall for my trick to go to Clark AFB again. I was stuck for the day.

I had a flying buddy 29 August: LCDR Hewitt. He was a founding member of the Saints (an original member of the squadron when formed and known as a "plank owner"). He was now flying an A-7 assigned to VA-82 on the *USS America*. He was a really nice guy. We flew at 0.82 Mach speed and made a quick trip out of it. He had a Charlie (landing) time to make while I had some flex in my arrival.

I filled several roles on 30 August that changed as the day wore on. Being the Hanna, everything was late; we were assigned to be the noon-to-midnight carrier and were behind right from the start. My first mission was changed from an armed-recce flight to a RESCAP flight. After everyone cleared, my wingman and I went in and hit a bridge. My second hop of the day was to be the last tanker launched, but that changed several times to a spare tanker mission when a VA-55 tanker went down. I was on the Cat and my bird went down.

Then I was assigned a night mission that got cancelled because two of our birds diverted to Chu Lai.

I finally launched at 2347 having been up since 0800. As the tanker and only aircraft launched, I was sent to bring our F-8 CAP (Combat Air Patrol) back to the ship. I headed out to the Do Son peninsula to pick up LCDR John Bartocci and his wingman. It turned out to be a mission easier said than done.

The night was very dark, no stars to be seen, no moon, no lights on the water and of course the Vietnamese did not turn on lights at night, that only invited an attack. I turned off my radios and my instrument lights and felt as if I were floating in some dark, alien space. There was something electric about it. I could feel the tingling through my arm down to my hands and into the stick. I knew that it would be no ordinary night.

We are graced to meet some special souls in this life, and this is one such story. John was a friend, a gentleman and a fine naval aviator whose life was lost on a night approach to a 27-Charlie WWII-type carrier in the South China Sea. A small-deck carrier for the F-8 to land on. I almost lost my life that same evening.

John and I ate together in the wardroom that morning: both of us had flown night missions and caught a late breakfast. We had become good friends despite the fact that he was an "F-8 Crusader Pilot – last of the gunfighters" and I a simple "air to mud" pilot flying an A-4. Previously, the two of us had carried out a scheme where we launched as a team working the countryside as if we were a pair of A-4s. We trolled for MIGs, hoping that the appeal of attacking two, overloaded A-4s flying without fighter protection would be irresistible. Even though we got a few tentative bites, we never got the MIGs to engage. But that's straying from the story.

After breakfast, while playing a couple of games of Acey-Deucy, John mentioned that he had a double cycle (flying a three-hour shift instead of the normal 1 ½ hrs.) launch for the last cycle that night. I told him I was on the schedule to be the duty A-4 "pump," in-flight refueling aircraft and would cover the last launch and recovery. We anticipated having some time "up close and personal" during the night.

As I rendezvoused with John and his wingman, they needed some fuel to get them back and for the approach. The wingman was the first to try to refuel. The F-8 is a very hard aircraft to refuel in daylight conditions and refueling off the small A-4 at night is almost impossible. It was as challenging as trying to park your Ford Expedition in you grandma's single-car garage with your eyes closed!

The less-than-ordinary evening continued with John's wingman sliding under my right wing and pulling up, almost resulting in a mid-air engagement of the worst kind. After a couple of tries, both of them were refueled and they flew off my wing back to the carrier.

As we approached the carrier, I dropped the wingman off at about 6 miles and John and I continued on to the 2-mile fix where he called the ball. I slid to John's left so I wouldn't interfere with his approach but where I would be in a position for him to come up for a quick "drink" of fuel if he happened to "bolter" (a missed landing). It had already been a long day for John, and he didn't like having to make night, carrier landings in the F-8. John boltered. He stated he didn't need a ' drink," so I made a hard-left turn to get back in position to cover the wingman's approach.

The wingman fared no better, but he did need a "drink." His fuel state was getting low, and his voice was sounding more strained. Night carrier landings were stressful enough when you had plenty of fuel; being short of fuel raised his stress level.

As he hooked up, I turned us down wind so that I would be in a position to cover John's next approach while getting the wingman in position for his approach. A-4 jocks were "Full-service tankers."

As the wingman finished refueling, I made another hard-left turn, put the nose down and added power so I could catch up to John who was now about a mile out. As John approached the ramp, I was slightly behind him on his left side looking at his aircraft when he suddenly exploded into this large fireball sliding down the deck. John had hit the ramp, the end of the flight deck. As his aircraft slid down the deck in flames, the engine and cockpit broke loose and went over the side into the water; the rest of the plane was in flames on the flight deck.

The ship became a beehive of frantic activity; flashlights were sent over the side to mark the spot in the water where pieces of airplane and maybe a pilot had gone. Fire-fighting crews fought the fire on the flight deck, "pri-fly" (our control tower) asked for fuel status and informed the wingman and me that our signal was now "bingo Chu Lai" (go land in South Viet Nam).

There was only one problem with that plan: not enough fuel for the both of us to "bingo Chu Lia." Calls were made to the *USS Constellation*, the "Connie" as we knew her, to see if they could do an emergency pull-forward to recover us. They could, but it would be about 45 to 60 minutes, and that would be too long. There was only one solution. I topped off the wingman, he flew on to Chu Lia, and I climbed to altitude and held to see if they could get me a "clear deck" before I ran out of fuel.

As I climbed to altitude, I wasn't sure what I felt. I had just seen a good friend and aviator die. I was stunned and had thoughts of John as I had known him. He was lively and caring, but I could not spare the time to reflect on John as I would have liked. I faced an approach with minimal fuel.

Through the clouds below I could see activity on the flight deck. The fire-fighting crews and the flight-deck crews knew I was up there and that my life might depend on their ability to get the deck clear as soon as possible. Time was moving forward, and my own fuel gauge was reading lower and lower. Finally, the call: "Old Salt 1, Charlie." (The ship was now ready for me to land).

My fuel gauge read "0," so I had to power back as I circled down. In my mind the aim point for the approach was about a half mile to a mile astern the ship at an altitude of between 150 and 300 feet. The closer to the ship, the lower I needed to be, but I had to arrest the descent without adding power. Fuel was critical and power uses fuel. I slammed down the gear handle, dropped the hook and I was ready to "call the ball." I had been sucking down the oxygen, my throat was dry, and all I could say was "Salt 1, fuel zero."

I knew the LSO from his voice, and it was calming to hear, "Got you Mule, left for line up." Just as I thought I had it made, the ship started to disappear. At first it was just the bow, then the island, then the ball. I guess I cried out something like I lost the ship, but that calming voice came back saying, "I got your lights Mule, keep it coming." I checked my instruments; I felt the "burble" (the disturbed air caused by the ship's tower) and added power, I thought.

I heard the call of "Power," then the radio quit, and I looked out and saw the ball dropping, turning red, the wave off lights began flashing and I began to think how quiet it was, with no engine noise when I slammed into the deck. I never hit so hard in my life. As the airplane rocked forward, bouncing, I really didn't comprehend what was happening. Then the hook caught, and I slammed forward into my harness. That slam never felt so good; it meant I was home.

As I came to rest, the white deck lights came on, and saw that shipmates had crammed every lookout spot to watch for my arrival. Men were running up to the aircraft; my plane captain opened the canopy and yelled at the top of his lungs. I think they were happy we didn't lose "another one" that night. So was I!

The LSO and I walked to the edge of the flight deck and sat there looking at the night sea. I've always felt the calming effect of the ship moving through the water, the sight of the luminescence of the water at night as it curled away from the ship, the sound of the water slapping against the hull. We both needed that calming effect. He had never "lost one" before and had never "waved" one that had flamed out. We didn't talk much; we both deeply felt the loss of a friend.

As we sat there, he explained why the ship disappeared. The ship was streaming black smoke from the boilers. When the ship went to full emergency stop to look for John, the nozzles of the oil burners coked over so when they had to go full steam ahead to get 30 knots of wind over the deck for my landing, the coke burned off leaving a heavy smoke trail. Since it was night, I couldn't see the smoke trail, and, even if I had known it was there, I would have had to fly through it to recover.

John was a very good pilot. From my own experience, being good isn't enough. You also had to be lucky. Today, I still ponder what it is that makes one lucky. Certainly, John was a good person, well liked and respected. It wasn't enough. I have no idea why I was the lucky one or why luck has been with me through some other close calls. I can only say that I was very lucky!

It was now 31 August and time to get to bed. It was the anniversary of when we lost Dave, Al, and Dick Perry. And this year we lost John. Not a very lucky date for sure. Due to the extended previous day and our loss, it was a stand-down day. There was an AOM for the squadron, but thankfully no flying. I didn't need to get airborne considering how long my day had been and how it had ended.

The Hanna had a propensity for FUBAR days, and 1 September was a good example. Red Crown (a radio monitoring ship) had determined that "Woody" Woods, one of our squadron pilots, had some kind of emergency. In actuality he did not, but this started the fun. Watching the ensuing mess was like a Keystone Cops movie. They started to move all the aircraft forward to clear the landing area for Woody and then received the message that there was no emergency. Now we had airplanes moving in both directions and ship 315, in which I was sitting made three trips up and down the flight deck without the use of an engine. My flight was cancelled of course.

I stole a late, tanker hop. The cat shot was soft, and I barely got airborne. A bit of touch and go using ground effect that kept me flying until I had enough speed to climb. We now had three tankers airborne with nearly 22,000 pounds of fuel in total. We had only one F-8 to recover, and he wouldn't use that much fuel in three, complete missions. Another Keystone Cops scenario due to poor communication. What a way to end the day.

I had three hops on 2 September. The first was an armed recce flight, during which I was hit by a 37mm gunner and sustained some holes in my canopy and my vertical fin on the front. I was in my diving run on the target and he was either a good shot or just got lucky. My plane captain found a piece of the 37mm shell in my headrest and gave it to me, I call it my good luck charm and still have it. The second hop was a smaller than usual Alpha to Noi Hoi. Our leader apparently didn't know how to read the jungle ground of North Vietnam because we never got there. Nonetheless, we did drop our bombs on North Vietnam, which accomplished our goal for the day.

My third was a test hop which is always a lot of fun when the aircraft checks out okay. I took a little extra time and burned extra fuel making some low passes by the ship. The first pass was at about 20 feet, which created a nice rooster tail behind my jet. The second was at flight-deck level down the port side of the ship, which gave the crew, a good look at the airplane as I was close aboard. The ship's Captain wasn't impressed but what could he do? Send me to Vietnam? I was already here, so instead I got a good lecture. I got two "OK" landings and one "(OK)" or fair landing.

The next morning, we finally got to Noi Hoi and dropped our bombs as required. I blew my landing with a "(OK)" fair landing. Due to a previous NG landing (No grade), I was now behind Step by .05 points.

The weather cancelled all flying 4 September, and I had to settle for second-place money. It was my own fault for getting that NG landing. Since there was no flying, we headed toward Cubi for R&R. It was an anti-climactic end to our first On the Line period, which was much different from last year.

We just were not effective doing what we were supposed to be doing. As our old Skipper would say, we were wasting tax-payer money. I agreed. On the positive side, we weren't losing pilots.

CHAPTER THIRTY-EIGHT

Cubi R&R: 1968

The normal sailing time between Yankee Station and Cubi Point, Philippines, was about three days. We left Yankee early in September because of weather.

The next day was spent running the deck, allowing the new guys get in landing practice. Not a good show, many messed up their approaches with a lot of wave-offs. They really needed the practice.

We arrived on the 6th and were able to get to the Officers' Club for dinner and drinks. Just getting off the ship was nice.

I had shore patrol duty in Olongapo; that and a then standing an SDO kept me out of trouble. We had four days in port. On one of those days, we organized a basketball game against our troops. The officers won 47- 36, but all of us had some sore muscles and blistered feet. It was a fun game, enjoyed by all.

The ship left port 11 September bound for Yankee Station. I flew aboard and got an "OK" pass. I flew a night training hop with a wingman who was practicing several night rendezvous. After some fun night flying, I returned to the ship and got another "OK."

It was a good start on the landing scoreboard.

The next two days were enroute to Yankee without much to do. It was very boring and made the days seem very long.

CHAPTER THIRTY-NINE

Second On Line Period

W e were back at Yankee Station, and I had two hops on 14 September. The first was a mission using snake-eye fins on 500-pound bombs.

The bombs were fused to function as mines, and we seeded the rivers to stop movement. The fins would open like an X, retarding the bomb and landed at the target after we passed. We made our passes at about 200 feet above the ground. It was a good trip but small-arms, ground fire left my plane with a small hole.

On the second hop, I was the wingman for LCDR Dean "Dynamite" Cramer. He was a crusty, older veteran from our '67 cruise. Dynamite was a good pilot, but not always a lot of fun to fly with. We found a beautiful boat, about 120-180 feet long. It looked like a fast boat. We both hit it, but it didn't catch fire or sink; both of us were a bit disappointed. I don't think it was serviceable anymore, so we did accomplish something.

As for my landings I got another "OK" but a dreaded "NG" which hurt my score. But it was my fault, no one else to blame.

I woke up at 0400 on 15 September to fly the first of three-hops. I was lead with LTJG Dick "Greasy" Harriss on my wing. It was a dark launch with an early-light recovery. We found some trucks and got them burning, but it had become harder to find any movement in any of the areas assigned to us. Most of the materiel movement now occurred through Laos.

My second mission was to Tam Da with LTJG. Scottie "Fat-boy" Mitchell. As we approached, they unloaded on us with several 37mm guns but did no damage. We hit our target well.

The third mission was a test hop, which went well. The aircraft checked out and passed all the required tests. Once again, I had fun giving the troops a little airshow which is a nice break from the normal routine. I landed about 1850 to complete a long day. I did get three "OK" passes so that helped my average.

We had a RESCAP mission the next morning. When all the planes were feet wet, we were released to go hunting. We didn't find anything but worn-out bridges. It was ridiculous bombing here in the North when we could have been helping out in the south protecting our boys.

Our XO, CDR Ed Shropshire, took a hit in the cockpit. It did some damage to the cockpit including his radio control. He came in without flaps and did a great job on recovery but had sustained a cut to his neck, so he had some blood on his flight suit. We were glad it was not worse; he was one of the "Good Guys."

I flew an early, armed-recce with Jello on 17 September. Upon return, I felt horrible and checked with the doc. I spent the next four days in sickbay fighting the flu. Sickbay was not R&R.

I had a weather-recon early in the morning on 22 September with Baron on my wing and called back the weather at various checkpoints. It wasn't the most exciting type of mission, but, as my first flight since falling sick, it was fine. I made a mess of the landing and only got an "(OK)" fair pass. Some days were diamonds and some days were stones.

I flew a RESCAP with Jello on 23 September when a pilot from VA-55 off the Hanna went down. We got to the area where he went down, saw a blackened area that was still smoking but didn't hear any beeper. There was a 23mm, four-gun battery firing at us. I was loaded with Zunis and Jello had bombs. I thought I got some good hits with my Zunis, but he kept firing. Jello made some good drops, but that guy still unloaded on us until we had to leave. I guess he won that engagement.

That same day a VA-106 pilot, landing on the *USS Intrepid* hit the LSO platform and killed the LSO, an enlisted crew member (the LSO recorder) and himself.

My second hop was a night launch, so we were dropping bombs under illumination provided by flares. Not the most strategic day, other than my landings, which were two "OK" passes.

We got some good news the next morning. The North Vietnamese released a statement that they had captured an A-4 pilot. The ship intelligence officers felt that my staying in the area for such a long period indicated that I had contact with the downed pilot. I didn't, but knowing he survived was good. I was scheduled for another two-hop day on the 24th. The first flight was with both Dynamite and Felter.

After we got to the target, I lost my radios and my ability to communicate. Since I couldn't communicate, I dropped my full load and flew back to the ship. I learned later that my abrupt departure greatly annoyed Dynamite; as he didn't know what happened to me, but then how was I supposed to tell him about my problem?

The second hop was with Gary Beck and went just fine. We got a couple of trucks in "Happy Valley," so that made our day. Even better was that I got two "OK" landings.

My turn at SDO came up 25 September. The main goal was to keep the rabble (our pilots) doing their jobs, and make sure the chair in which I sat did not fly up and hit the ceiling. Really not hard duty and nobody shooting at me.

Author as Squadron Duty Officer. Photo by "Jello" Groff.

On 26 September we became the noon-to-midnight carrier. I had an early go with LTJG Gordy Reed on my wing. We flew to just the north of Vinh to attract their attention. We encountered a few 37mm guns that shot at us, and then we flew north along Highway 15. Nothing was moving so we went after a couple of old bridges that seemed to be under repair. That put them back to work for a while. Gordy and I had a nice, clear but still dark night hop; after launch I lost my radio; we dumped our unarmed bombs into the sea and circled the ship for over an hour before recovering. What a wasted night.

The next day was another three-hop day. The advantage of being a maintenance test pilot is getting an additional flight chance. I had a noon launch for a maintenance hop. The plane passed all the tests. With pri-fly's approval, I put on another air show for the crew. It boosted the morale of the hard-working sailors on the flight deck to see some of the capabilities of our jets. My second hop was RESCAP duty with Jello on my wing. We both had a gun pod centerline and I found an oil barge. We left it in flames. My last hop had LTJG Bob "Bullet" Senecal on my wing. It was a nice clear night but there was nothing moving and nothing we could find under our flares. I guess we just made more holes in the ground. Two "OK" and one "(OK)" landings rounded my day. Overall, when including the air show, a good, fun day.

The Hanna flipped to the midnight-to-noon carrier on 28 September. I briefed at 0100 for a tanker mission, but my plane went down as I was strapped to the cat. I was assigned as a spare for a 0430 launch, but no one went down. I was and up all night and ended up doing nothing. A wasted night and day.

I was the SDO again the next evening starting at midnight. I spent the entire 12 hours keeping everyone happy. No flying so that meant another wasted day, because I did enjoy flying.

Going from noon-to-midnight designation to midnight-to-noon on successive days meant 24 hours of duty, so 30 September was a stand-down day. Twenty-four hours of duty did take some steam out of us, so a day off was a good chance to recover. Thirty-one days of duty aboard the Hanna remained for me. I was short; I had not received orders, but the Navy would have to send me somewhere.

My first hop on 1 October was a tanker: a black, night launch and a black, dark recovery. My second hop was an armed-recce flight at sunrise with LTJG Dick "Greasy" Harriss. It was a seeder hop, where we dropped snake eyes in the river as mines. We ended up having mock dogfights with two A-6 Intruders off the *USS America*. We won two of the dogfights but lost the last one. Greasy hung in there as a good wingman covering his leader. A dogfight requires that you fly the aircraft, pushing it to the edge or even over the edge of the flight envelope. To do that is a good feeling; I really enjoyed pushing the envelope. As far as landings, I received one "OK" and one "(OK):" not that bad on landings.

The Hanna had a bad day on 2 October. Three aircraft were damaged (one from VA-55 and two from VA-164). Commander Erwin, the XO from VA-164, was hit near Vinh. After he got feet wet, with his plane on fire, he ejected. He was not seen again, but his chute and helmet were spotted in the surf. He was listed as KIA.

I watched as the moon set on 3 October and then was launched into a black, black night. I was the duty tanker. Fortunately, everything went smoothly.

My second hop was an armed recce with Jello. We had no significant engagements with no real shooting, per se. Upon approach to the ship, Jello and I engaged in two, short dogfights; we won both so that made me happy.

I was on the schedule for a 0200 brief the next morning, so I headed to my bed for some rest. I was awakened by the 1MC (The ships self-powered intercom) stating "Pilot in the water, starboard side."

LT Jim Merrick of our photo squadron, VFP-63, spun in during a mock dogfight. He was another KIA so another wasted pilot. Those last two days in a row reminded me of how bad October of last year was.

The next day our bad luck ended; we didn't lose anyone. I had my usual two-hop, night-day schedule; we transitioned to the noon-to-midnight carrier and another 24-hour stretch of duty. They were very ordinary hops with an "OK" for both the night and day landings, so I was happy.

I started 5 October on an easy, day hop with Gordy on my wing. I had a second daylight hop as a RESCAP with a gun pod on centerline. I didn't find much moving but strafed another barge in the river. It must have been empty because it didn't sink or catch fire. I got another "OK" and a fair grade on my landings so not a bad day after all.

By this time, I now had over 200 missions over the North, but 6 October was my turn to commit a stupid, rookie mistake. The first hop with Greasy was an easy daylight armed recce. The North Vietnamese knew we were around so nothing much was moving. We did see some undamaged rail cars and proceeded to damage them.

The rail cars author and his wingman found. Author's bomb on target.

On the second hop, Jello and I launched with daylight, but it was to be a nighttime recovery. On launch we still had some sunlight up at altitude that gave us a visible horizon, which made it less stressful.

We were loaded with five, 500-pound bombs, three flares and a 400-gallon, centerline, fuel tank. We had more than enough fuel for a 1 hour, 45-minute mission. As it got darker, we would use the flares to light up the ground so we could find targets to bomb. I would rather have had some 5-inch, Zuni rockets between us to help hit the anticipated trucks, but we did with what we were given.

As we approached the beach, it was starting to get dark at ground level while at altitude we had the setting sun giving us plenty of light. We had just intercepted Route 1 and begun our briefed track, when I spotted two trucks trying to hide underneath some trees. They were also using a small village to help conceal themselves, but I had them.

I was down at 1,000 feet above the ground to see better any movement while Jello my wingman was up at 10,000 feet ready to roll in on the target. I gave visual directions to help him spot the trucks and drop a bomb on them. I began my climb to altitude so that I could follow up Jello's run, but Jello was unable to use my directions to spot the target. I told him to circle. I would tell him when I began my run and that he could spot my bomb going off and use the explosion to guide him to the target. I got to altitude, rolled in, and dropped on the trucks. As I pulled off, I saw that I hit close to them, but I didn't set either of them on fire. I asked Jello if he had seen my bomb detonate; he replied that he had not.

This frustrated me a bit. I didn't want to waste much time on these two trucks, and certainly not more than one or two bombs. I had expended one of my bombs and didn't feel like trying another so I told Jello I would make another pass and use my guns. He could follow the tracers from my bullets to identify the target.

As I got to roll-in altitude the sun had not yet set. I looked down at the ever-darkening ground and started my run. I couldn't find those trucks. Going from the light into the dark had affected my night vision. Where were they?

It was a moment that I will never forget. The view from my cockpit was dark mother earth. It filled my cockpit canopy, and I realized that I was in trouble. I pulled the power back to idle, and I rolled in all the back trim I had. I wasn't going to quit so I pulled hard, harder than I had ever pulled before. Slowly my picture began to change, and the tree and trucks came into my view. The tree was towering over me, big and getting bigger by the fractions of a second. The trucks loomed large and ever closer.

Suddenly night turned into day. Off to my right front a 37mm gun fired. The muzzle blast illuminated the area like a flare: I could see I was level with the front doors of houses in the village, and I could see inside them. The firing scared the hell out of me.

Reflexively I relaxed the pressure I had on the stick. This was not the thing to do; I was still too low and not gaining any altitude, but I couldn't believe they shot at me. First of all, the shell wouldn't have had time to arm in that short of distance and I was flying past the gun at almost 450 kts. What kind of an idiot would take that shot? Of course, while I was thinking this, and I had relaxed the pressure on the stick. I had come to the end of the clearing around the village.

I could feel the airplane hitting the trees. That woke me up! I was in deep trouble, and I had to get back to flying quickly or I wasn't going to be able to go home. As I fought with the airplane, I asked Jello, "Did you see that @#%% shoot at me?" He responded that he did, and I calmly told him to bomb the living @#%% out of that area. "Drop all your bombs, I'm in trouble."

Jello did a good job. There was a large fire where the trucks had been, and I told him to join me on the way out. As it turned out, other aircraft saw the fires and more of them bombed the area that night. When I returned the next day, I found several other trucks burned as well as the gun.

The trouble I had (due to a stupid rookie mistake) was re-solved; the trouble I would have with the Skipper had just begun. Fortunately, I was able to be recovered on the ship. The aircraft had quite a bit of damage; the trees relieved my airplane of the bombs, centerline tank, and there were branches everywhere. The Skipper was not very happy with me.

It is common knowledge that many who have had a near-death experience talk of their life passing before their eyes. Since being a Navy Attack pilot is not a normal profession, I guess I shouldn't have expected a normal experience. All I could think of was how stupid I was.

The "air to mud" (dive bombing) pilots were schooled to avoid target-fixation ever since bombs were first carried by pilots or planes. It has been said that experience is the best teacher, and I was well-taught by that experience.

I had two hops the next day, but all we really did was make more holes in the ground. On the positive side I had two "OK" land-ings; a wasted day but one day shorter.

We stood down on 8 October to allow us to catch up on some needed sleep. I used the time to make certain that I had pictures of our entire crew.

I got orders that day as well. I would leave the *USS Hancock* on 1 November and report to VF-126 stationed at US Navy base Miramar in San Diego, California as of 1 December 1968. San Diego was definitely a step up from Lemoore, California. I had been to San Diego for survival school and liked the city, so I thought it was a good deal for me.

The next day, 9 October, we continued with our noon-to-midnight schedule. We were briefed that we would continue with this schedule until the 14th when would leave the line for R&R. We would fly the planes off to Cubi and be there for about five days.

From there we would be going to Singapore, which was a new city for me. We all got excited, but first, we had to get through another five days of missions. I had two hops that day. The first hop was with Jello to Happy Valley. Some guy decided to shoot at us, so we bombed him. Although he was following orders, it was the last decision he made in his time on earth.

The night hop with Greasy was up near Than Hoa, but we didn't find much movement. I got two "OK" landings and was at the top the landing board.

From 10 October until the 14th was mainly a repeat of the previous days. My wingmen varied, but the results of the missions not so much. I did get a couple of holes in my jet on the 13th, just bad luck on an unlucky day, even if it was a Sunday. I won the landing pot, and I was a happy camper. A 31-day stretch on the line was one of the longer ones of my Vietnam tour; it was nice that it wasn't as intense as last year.

During this last week of flying, I tried to imprint on my mind the sights of Saints flying around the ship and the approaches for landings. Those last missions were likely to be my last carrier operations and I would no longer be considered a carrier-qualified pilot. The icing on the cake was winning the landing pot as I finished my carrier career. The cake was the fact that I had survived my combat tour. I didn't have an answer to why I survived when so many of my friends didn't. I knew I would miss the intense feelings I had during our '67 period, but I also knew I didn't want to go back there again.

CHAPTER FORTY

On to Singapore

I off-loaded a plane on 15 October and flew into Cubi. I would have a couple of days of good food and drink before the ship's scheduled arrival on the 17th.

Step, Baron, Fat Boy, and I found ways to fill our bellies with food and drink. Cubi had few things to offer, but we had some good times. We were all looking forward to Singapore.

We sailed out of Cubi 22 October for our new destination. I was selected as one of several to fly planes out to the ship because we would be loading all of our aircraft aboard. I also had to do a maintenance flight on the way. The plane passed all of the required checks, and there was time for a few dogfights. I had more time in the A-4 than most of the others and won the fights I was in.

The ship, on its way to Singapore, diverted farther south so we could cross the equator. Most of the pilots had never crossed the equator, so we were known as Pollywogs. As we crossed, we would have to go through an old Naval ritual of becoming Shellbacks. It is an old sailing tradition going back over 400 years. We had to prove we were worthy of being sons of Neptune, the God of the Sea and protector of seamen. We weren't quite sure what the ritual would be, but it was scheduled for 24 October and we looked forward to it.

There were many Shellbacks among the shipboard crew including an old chief with a big belly. After crawling through what appeared to be food scraps with many potato skin peels, we emerged to the chief, portraying Neptune's baby, and had to kiss his belly in order to become a Shellback. We had a great time, and the Hanna now had a full complement of Shellbacks as we headed to Singapore.

We arrived in Singapore on 25 October. It still was a British protectorate, so the currency was the English pound and a bit more expensive than Japan. We had been invited to a dinner hosted by a Royal Navy Flight Squadron. They were presently deployed, but the wives and families gave us a very warm and friendly reception. They arranged for a tour of the city and a special visit to Boogie Street. Boogie Street was famous for the most beautiful women walking the street. In truth they were transvestites, but they did look like very gorgeous women. It was a very nice evening, and we had a great time.

The next few days were all fun and included a going-away party for "Mule." Since it wasn't the Philippines or on a US base, it wasn't as wild as other going-away parties, but it was a lot of fun and a fitting end for me.

CHAPTER FORTY-ONE

Homeward Bound

The Hanna headed to Yankee on 1 November with all my friends. I bid them all good luck.

I was bundled aboard the COD (Carrier Airborne Delivery plane) and flown to the Philippines to begin my trip back to the United States. I flew back on a Trans World Airways 707 and arrived in San Francisco on 5 November, election day. I went to bed after a long trip home and awoke to a new President-elect. President Johnson was not on the ballot. I reported to VF-126 on 1 December.

San Diego was good duty. I met a nice lady there and married her after I left the Navy in February, 1970. I wanted to stay in California, but there were no jobs available. I was fortunate to be hired by Delta Air Lines. I would spend 32 years flying various routes and jets before retiring in 2002 at the mandatory retirement age of 60.

Because of my friendship with LCDR Bill Rankin and my guilt for not intervening to prevent his death, I became an active member of the Delta Air Line Pilots Association (ALPA) safety committee. I participated in many areas, one of which included investigation of accidents and incidents involving airplanes.

I participated in the investigation of two major accidents at Delta. I later became the chairman of the safety committee and, through that committee participated in major changes to aviation safety in the United States.

My former squadron mate, Admiral James Busey, was appointed head of the FAA. Through his efforts and those of several of my committee members we were able to change the way departures were flown to mitigate noise levels, but also to ensure that safety standards were maintained.

That problem arose because airlines were being denied service if they broke the local noise ordinance flying out of John Wayne airport in California. The noise restrictions led to power reductions after taking off such that, if an aircraft lost power on one engine, it would more than likely crash before the aircraft could regain enough power to sustain flight.

In addition to the noise issue, Adm. Busey challenged me and my team to get the pilots to accept a Flight Operations Quality Assurance (FOQA) program in the United States.

Similar programs were being put in place in other countries to enhance flight safety. After a lot of work, we were able to convince pilots of all the airlines to accept this program. It used flight data to show where mistakes were made in flight operations.

These mistakes were analyzed as to their causes. The results from this analysis were used for training purposes to ensure pilots would be aware of these mistakes and correct them before they happened. This program is the cornerstone for our safety efforts today. It was ironic that it took ten years to convince the FAA lawyers to give up their power and allow this program to proceed.

We worked with many human-factor experts to develop a better cockpit environment, Crew Resource Management (CRM), where the captain would solicit input from other crew members for solutions to problems and encourage other crew members to inform the captain if they saw a problem.

Many other safety programs were initiated that led to the United States aviation system being the safest travel system in the world.

Above, author on the left investigates Swissair 111 crash, and below he stands on the left with U.S. Navy investigators.

My last safety job was being the International Federation of Air Line Pilots Association (IFALPA) lead investigator in the crash of Swissair 111 in September,1998. I had a great team of pilot investigators from two Canadian airlines as well as six pilots representing Swissair.

We worked with the Transportation Safety Board (TSB) of Canada for four years to determine what happened to the aircraft. We were able to make changes in a pilot's response to the presence of smoke in the cockpit as well as circuit breaker design, wire insulation and FAA regulations regarding aircraft design.

It was a long journey, but the tragedy of Bill Rankin's death influenced me to make airline safety a priority in my career. Godspeed, Bill.

Only the dead have seen the end of war.

George Santayana

Afterword

It has been 55 years since I first went to war. Just as it has done for those soldiers, sailors and marines who went to war before I went to mine, the world has moved on.

Enemies become friends and allies. Countries become trading partners. My New Balance shoes that I wear are made in the unified Vietnam. I have met with a North Vietnamese pilot I flew against, in San Diego USA and escorted him on a tour of the carrier *USS Midway*. He was the only MiG 17 Ace of their air force and an acclaimed Hero of The Peoples Republic of Vietnam, so honored by Ho Chi Minh.

Even though the world had moved on and my memories had faded, when I re-read my diary, which is the foundation for this book, it brought back those moments of heart pounding fear, those days of mourning lost friends and the thoughts of how we were just seconds away from dying at any time.

The pace of operations was the most concentrated it has ever been for US carrier operations. That was one of the main reasons why I wanted to write the book. Another was to honor all my squadron and air wing mates who took this job seriously and put their lives on the line for their family, friends, and country. Any war veteran will give you the same description of the bonding between your platoon, company, or squadron. A bond that is still strong after all these years. When we do have our reunions, the love for one another is the strongest feeling along with the respect we have for each other.

We lost five members of my squadron in 1967 and we have three returned for burial, two in 1993, LCDR. Don Davis and LTJG Skip Foulks. LTJG Ralph Bisz, my roommate whose remains were returned 41 years after his death, was interred at Arlington National Cemetery in 2008. His immediate family was no longer with us, but we, his squadron family, were there. Most of us had a POW bracelet with his name engraved which we then had put in his casket to be buried with him. That is how strong our bonding is. We still have two of my squadron over in Vietnam. LT Jeff Krommenhoek was my wingman and I saw the missile hit him in a massive explosion. They found parts of his airplane and parts of his gear but no human remains, so his body will remain there forever.

LTJG James "Dools" Dooley my former roommate went down in Haiphong harbor, and the recovery teams have not as yet looked for his remains so we do not know if he will be returned.

I still think of these men every day, and whenever I give one of my PowerPoint presentations on the air war, I show my audience their pictures and tell their backgrounds so that they will not be forgotten. I won't let them be forgotten. They gave their all.

I was fortunate to survive the combat, and it is hard to think that some of the most important parts of my life happened in such a short number of years and so long ago.

I was twenty-four years old when I flew my first combat mission and twenty-six when I flew my last. It is hard to think today that I was ever that young.

I can say that it was an exciting life and a challenging one. The main thing I learned was that you had to have your mind in control at all times. If you became distracted, lost control of your emotions for just a second, it was your last second. Unfortunately, I saw that happen more than once, and that was the margin we lived in for those three years.

Skipper Bryan "Magnolia" Compton was the most ferocious warrior I have ever met. The pressure of losing as many pilots as we did—five KIA, three severe injuries and three POW's out of the eighteen we left the USA with, plus two replacement pilots—caused that good leader to lose weight.

At his All-Officers Meetings in the ready room, he would stand there with his belt wrapped one and a half times around him, rub the scar on his nose and urge us on, telling us we had to keep the bomb pipper, that guidance indicator for aiming our bombs—on the target. "Stop wasting the taxpayer's money and hit the damn target."

He was an aggressive pilot which led to my following his example and working to become an aggressive pilot. I truly believe that is why I survived.

The Skipper went on to be the first Captain of the USS Nimitz, and then was promoted to Rear Admiral before retiring.

Several others from the squadron continued on having distinguished Navy careers. It is or at least was the most highly decorated Squadron in the history of the US Navy and I have always felt fortunate to have served in it.

Appendix A- Navy Officer Ranks

O-1   Ensign   **ENS**
Same as 2nd Lieutenant United States Marine Corp (USMC)

O-2   Lieutenant Junior Grade   **LTJG**
Same as 1st Lieutenant United States Marine Corp (USMC)

O-3   Lieutenant   **LT**
Same as Captain United States Marine Corp (USMC)

O-4   Lieutenant Commander   **LCDR**
Same as Major United States Marine Corp (USMC)

O-5   Commander   **CDR**
Same as Lieutenant Colonel United States Marine Corp (USMC)

O-6   Captain   **CAPT**
Same as Colonel United States Marine Corp (USMC)

O-7	**Commodore**	**RDML**	**1 Star**
O-8	**Rear Admiral**	**RADM**	**2 Star**
O-9	**Vice Admiral**	**VADM**	**3 Star**
O-10	**Admiral**	**ADM**	**4 Star**
O-11	**Fleet Admiral**	**FADM**	**5 Star**
	Not used since 1966		

Appendix B- Carrier Operations in 1966-68

Flight operations for carriers in the '60s were different from the normal United States Air Force fighter operations. In both services fighters flew down the landing runway at a high speed and then "break," a steep left turn pulling several Gs, which slowed the airplane to enable dropping the landing gear and flaps. The aircraft turned until it was parallel to the landing runway, flying opposite the landing course.

In the carrier operations the aircraft were offset to starboard of the ship's course. The break was planned so that rolling out on the opposite course put the aircraft abeam the end of the moving ship, then commenced a left, descending turn to line up for landing. Following aircraft maintained a 30-second gap for landing. The daylight VFR (visual flying rules) was at an initial altitude of 600 feet above the water, where the normal airport altitude is usually 1500 feet above ground level.

Night carrier operations usually followed the same approach, if the weather allowed. When the weather would not allow the pattern to work, the pilots were assigned an altitude and a point in space defined by the ships TACAN. Each airborne aircraft would be at different assigned altitude. The pilot would follow the TACAN radial to the ship, leveling at 1200 feet above the water and fly level until sighting the glide slope, as displayed by the Fresnel lens ball. If waved off or a bolter, the aircraft climbed to 600 feet or an assigned altitude and followed the ship's radar guidance to get back in line for landing.

Night operations are not fun because the ship had minimal lighting other than the "ball," and usually there was no defined horizon. Just another challenge for a Naval Aviator.

About the Author:

Ken "Mule" Adams is a retired Delta Air Lines Pilot who lives with his wife Betsy in Cartersville Georgia. He is an accomplished sailor who has sailed in almost all the various waters around the world. After retiring, with the help of a Canadian friend, he built his first "stink boat" which he and Betsy lived on during the summers in Shediac, New Brunswick, Canada sailing the Northumberland Straight, Bras- d'Or in Cape Breton, Nova Scotia, Canada.

Over the years he's owned and built a series of light airplanes and started a flying museum of Liaison-type aircraft.

Manufactured by Amazon.ca
Bolton, ON

46465163R00164